PENGUIN BOOKS

KEEP YOUR BABY SAFE

Jane Asher is an established actress who has appeared in many productions on television, film and in the West End theatre. She is married to artist Gerald Scarfe and they have three children. Her father, Dr Richard Asher, was a highly respected consultant physician, admired not only for his medical skill but also for his brilliant writing and speaking.

She has written several successful books, including *Jane Asher's Party Cakes*, *Jane Asher's Fancy Dress*, *Easy Entertaining* and *The Moppy Stories* (for young children). Of her previous baby-care book, *Silent Nights for You and Your Baby*, the *Sunday Times* wrote, 'Any parent enduring the misery of sleepless nights with babies or toddlers will find the book both comforting and helpful', and Jane Asher was described by 9–5 magazine as 'an original and creative thinker in a field hitherto dominated by some tedious and bombastic child experts'. She hopes that this book will be equally helpful in preventing and treating some of the thousands of tragic accidents to babies that occur each year.

Since writing this book Jane Asher has been appointed a Trustee of the Child Accident Prevention Trust and is also involved with the Department of Transport in promoting the use of child car-restraints.

Comments from experts on
KEEP YOUR BABY SAFE

Pamela Davies, MD, FRCP (*Foundation of the Study of Infant Deaths*)

'Bravo! If you could persuade parents to try and do all these things, much needless anguish and disability would be avoided. I think your book should be very helpful.'

Vic Bagnelle (*London Fire and Civil Defence Authority*)

'The book is exellent and should be in arm's length of every mother with young children.'

Dr D. Zideman (*Hammersmith Hospital*)

'An authoritative guide and an excellent reference book on how to prevent and deal with accidents and emergencies in infants and children.'

Dr J. L. Kennerley Bankes, FRCS

'It is a very readable and practical guide which will give a lot of reassurance to many parents. There is sound common sense throughout and I expect it will have a wide readership.'

JANE ASHER

KEEP

YOUR BABY

SAFE

A GUIDE TO THE PREVENTION AND TREATMENT OF ACCIDENTS AND MEDICAL EMERGENCIES IN BABIES AND CHILDREN UP TO THREE

PENGUIN BOOKS

PENGUIN BOOKS

Published by the Penguin Group
27 Wrights Lane, London W8 5TZ, England
Viking Penguin Inc., 40 West 23rd Street, New York 10010, USA
Penguin Books Australia Ltd, Ringwood, Victoria, Australia
Penguin Books Canada Ltd, 2801 John Street, Markham, Ontario, Canada L3R 1B4
Penguin Books (NZ) Ltd, 182–190 Wairau Road, Auckland 10, New Zealand

Penguin Books Ltd, Registered Offices: Harmondsworth, Middlesex, England

First published by Penguin 1988

Filmset in 10/12 Linotron 202 Electra by
Wyvern Typesetting Ltd, Bristol

Made and printed in Great Britain by
Hazell Watson & Viney Ltd
Member of the BPCC Group
Aylesbury, Bucks

Text designed by Sonia Alexis

Dedicated to Katie, Alexander and Rory

CONTENTS

III. USEFUL INFORMATION

PREFACE

I like to think of myself as a reasonably careful, sensible mother, yet during the time I was researching this book, my five-year-old son fell and broke his elbow very badly and my three-year-old scalded his foot. In just a split second family life can change from being a mixture of its normal complaints, frustrations and joys to a time of pain, misery and guilt.

Most of the horrors I have had to discuss in this book will never happen to your baby: the vast majority of children grow up happily, safely and accident-free, but anything that can be done to prevent even the smallest of scrapes or bumps will make your life that bit less worrying and give you more time to enjoy the delights of bringing up your baby.

Nobody can make a house accident-proof – an inquisitive toddler can manage to hurt himself in the most inventive and extraordinary ways. My daughter used to twiddle her hair when going to sleep and on more than one occasion wove such an intricate knot that she appeared downstairs in tears with her hand inextricably joined to the back of her head and had to be cut free.

Equally, nobody could be expected to take every precaution I have mentioned in this book – only you will know which dangers may be particularly applicable to your house and your baby – but as so many accidents can be easily prevented it really is worth doing as much as you can. While writing this book I became aware of many risks I had unknowingly taken with my own children. There are several changes that can be made to your surroundings to eliminate the most obvious dangers and knowing what to do should an accident occur will give you great peace of mind and help to prevent panic in an emergency situation.

Most accidents happen because parents fail to appreciate the quickly changing development of the baby in terms of movement and behaviour and how this relates to every-day articles and situations. It's difficult to appreciate, particularly with a first baby, how quickly and suddenly the baby discovers a new skill such as turning over or crawling, or a new experiment such as stuffing everything in sight into his or her mouth . . .

I have referred to the baby as 'he' throughout the book. I have done this purely for the sake of simplicity: obviously all the advice applies equally to boys and girls. Parents of boys, however, should perhaps be doubly watchful: statistically boys suffer almost twice as many accidents as girls. I wasn't at all surprised to discover this during my research; our first-born was a daughter and we secretly prided ourselves on how successfully we had reared her to be gentle, careful and non-aggressive. Since having two boys I now know it had nothing whatever to do with our influence – the aggressive physical energy of our two little males took me quite unawares and I am only surprised the incidence of bashed heads or cut limbs is not even more frequent than it is.

This book concerns only babies and young children up to the age of about three. It's not that accidents or medical emergencies become less likely from three years onwards – on the contrary, they unfortunately continue to be only too frequent – but they change in character once babyhood is over. This is also *not* a baby health-care book. I have only referred to medical conditions which could possibly result in serious or life-threatening situations, or ones you might think could do so. It may also be wise to have a medical encyclopaedia in the house – I have always found it extremely useful, particularly for spotting the childhood infectious diseases you are bound to come across eventually.

The more you know about potential accidents and medical emergencies the less likely you will be to panic unnecessarily over small incidents. As your baby can sense immediately when you are upset or frightened, it's obviously a good idea to react as calmly and matter-of-factly as possible when he hurts himself: a bit of good old English stiff upper lip will stand him in good stead later. There are many times when a parent finds herself picking up a screaming toddler with a cheerful 'Oops-a-daisy, did you fall all the way down the stairs then?' when she's silently panicking that he's broken every bone in his body.

Every day babies and young children endure unnecessary pain and unhappiness through preventable accidents; if this book helps to avoid even a small amount of the suffering caused to them and their families, it will have been worthwhile.

ACKNOWLEDGEMENTS

I would like to thank the following for their invaluable help and support:

Divisional Officer V. Bagnelle, London Fire Brigade (North West Area).

Mr T. R. Bull, FRCS, Consultant Otolaryngologist.

Child Accident Prevention Trust.

The Foundation for the Study of Infant Deaths.

Royal Society for the Prevention of Accidents (RoSPA).

Mr J. L. Kennerley Bankes, FRCS, Consultant Ophthalmologist.

Mr Peter Neville, Animal psychologist at the Animal Behaviour Centre.

Mr Michael Smith, FRCS, Consultant Orthopaedic Surgeon.

Dr G. N. Volans, B.SC., MD, FRCP, Consultant Clinical Pharmacologist and Director of the National Poisons Information Service.

Dr David Zideman, B.SC., MB, BS, FFARCS, Consultant Anaesthetist and founder member of the Resuscitation Council.

Trish Burgess, who worked with me in sorting out the final manuscript.

Dr R. Hugh Jackson, MC, FRCP, for writing the Foreword.

xviii ACKNOWLEDGEMENTS

Special thanks to Dr Stanley Rom, MB, B.ch., MRCP (UK), Consultant Paediatrician, who checked and re-checked the manuscript for me and whose enthusiasm and professionalism were an inspiration.

FOREWORD

by Dr R. Hugh Jackson, MC, FRCP
Founder of the Child Accident Prevention Trust

One of the most important changes that has occurred in the pattern of children's health in the past decade has been the emergence of children's accidents as the major problem of child health after the age of one year. Not only are accidents the cause of more deaths than the next two commonest causes put together, but also those which do not lead to death are so frequent that about one in six of all our children have to attend the Accident and Emergency department of their local hospital every year. Such accidents obviously cause a great deal of distress and suffering to children and their parents and make considerable demands upon health services.

In the past few years the importance of trying to prevent these accidents has at last begun to receive the recognition that it warrants. The process of accident prevention can take effect in any or all of three main areas: by making the overall environment safer; by reducing the potential harm of specific features; and by protecting and supervising the child. In other words, accident prevention relies on education. Jane Asher's book makes a valuable contribution to this educational field.

It is concerned with the problem of the protection of any young child and with the management of any injuries he may sustain. Since young children spend a greater proportion of their time in the home than older children, it concentrates in the main on home accidents. Mothers generally have a predominant responsibility for the safety of their babies and toddlers and for the older child, and here they are helped to understand accidents in relation to their child's development and capabilities. They are given very practical advice about the home environment and the safety of products in it, and on the anticipation of changes in the child's behaviour which will increase the risk of an accident as he grows up.

Many booklets on accident prevention have been written by so-called experts in this field. Though expertise is sometimes necessary – and Jane Asher has been prepared to use it, particularly in the field of the resuscitation and emergency case of the injured child – one of the most important features of this book is that it has not been written by a professional expert. Jane Asher is a person of wisdom and experience, a mother of three children who has recognized and studied the problem and is anxious to share the views with others. Her great skill in communicating with people, either as an actress, TV or radio personality, or author, pervades the whole book, and mothers who heed her advice will have cause to be grateful to her.

CHIEF CAUSES OF ACCIDENTAL DEATH AND SERIOUS INJURY IN BABIES AND YOUNG CHILDREN

Over a million children attend casualty departments every year after preventable accidents, and a quarter of these are children under four years old. In one recently recorded year there were over 5,000 fatal accidents in British homes and 214 involved children under four. The causes break down as follows:

- Suffocation 65
- Scalds/burns 28
- Choking 24
- Fractures 18
- Cuts 11
- Concussion 8
- Poisoning 6
- Other 54

In the same year at least 36,000 children under five attended Accident and Emergency departments for suspected poisoning and at least 11,000 were admitted to hospital. The vast majority of suspected poisonings occur to children of three and under.

Accidents are the commonest cause of death in children over one year old.

HOW TO KEEP YOUR BABY SAFE

1. Read through the emergency section; then read and try to learn the resuscitation A-B-C, bleeding and choking sections – it could save your baby's life. I believe every parent should know how to resuscitate his or her child.

2. Read the section on accident prevention and put as much of it into practice as possible. A list of approved equipment and prices is given on page 167.

3. Keep a first-aid kit in the house (see page 81).

4. Have your doctor's and local Accident and Emergency (A and E) department's telephone number stuck by every telephone.

5. Find out the address of your local A and E department and check that you would know how to get there in an emergency. Make sure it is open 24 hours a day.

6. Consider the possibility of one parent taking a first-aid course (see page 130).

7. Never hesitate to contact your doctor if something is wrong: remember you know your baby better than anyone else. Don't be afraid to be insistent if you are not being taken seriously.

8. Look at the illustrations in this book: sources of danger are coloured grey.

WHEN TO CONSULT THE DOCTOR

The Foundation for the Study of Infant Deaths has published the following sensible suggestions:

- If you think your baby is ill, even without any obvious symptoms, contact your doctor.
- If your baby shows any of the following symptoms, especially if he has more than one, your doctor would expect you to ask for advice:

ALWAYS URGENT

- A fit or convulsion, or if your baby turns blue or very pale
- Quick, difficult or grunting breathing
- Exceptionally hard to wake or unusually drowsy or does not seem to know you

SOMETIMES SERIOUS

- Croup or a hoarse cough with noisy breathing
- Cannot breathe freely through his nose
- Cries in an unusual way or for an unusually long time, or you think your baby is in severe pain, particularly if it persists
- Refuses feeds repeatedly, especially if unusually quiet
- Vomits repeatedly
- Frequent loose motions especially if watery (diarrhoea). Vomiting and diarrhoea together can lead to excessive loss of fluid from the body and this may need urgent

treatment. Diarrhoea with blood in the motions is important

- Unusually hot or cold or floppy

EVEN IF YOU HAVE CONSULTED A DOCTOR, HEALTH VISITOR OR NURSE, IF BABY IS NOT IMPROVING OR IS GETTING WORSE WITHIN 24 HOURS, TELL YOUR DOCTOR AGAIN.

I.

PREVENTION

GENERAL SAFETY AWARENESS

CHOKING

For more than a hundred years medical literature has contained reports and warnings against giving foods such as nuts, raw carrots and sweets to children lacking molars to grind them. Manufacturers are obliged by law to issue warnings on toys and baby equipment about small pieces that may come off and cause choking but unfortunately there has been little similar attention paid to the dangers of certain foods. Only Sweden has legislated for labelling on children's food clearly indicating the age from which it is suitable. They also have a warning label on pre-packaged, shelled peanuts. I think we should all press for similar advice and warnings on children's food in this country. Meanwhile, although there are no 'safe' foods, there are some precautions that can be taken to minimize the hazards.

Young babies

☐ Never, never leave the baby alone while eating or drinking – even an apparently harmless substance can be regurgitated and cause choking. One nationwide American study showed that nearly two thirds of child deaths from asphyxiation were caused by inhaled vomit or regurgitated milk or juice.

☐ Don't 'prop feed' him with his bottle by wedging it in position so you don't have to hold it for him. Milk could flow too quickly into his mouth and choke him.

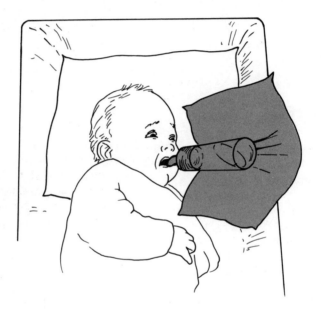

Solids

☐ Stick to relatively 'safe' foods that will dissolve in the mouth – proper baby rusks instead of biscuits, for example. Pieces of apple and carrot can be risky for children under two.

☐ Highly viscous foods, such as peanut butter, can mould to the airway and cause choking.

☐ From two onwards, apples and biscuits are safer, but hot dogs, grapes, nuts and sweets continue to be dangerous. The shape and texture of hot dogs give a clue to the types of food that can cause choking; they are the perfect round, pliable, compressible shape and texture to effectively form a plug in the airway. I remember once even an apparently harmless slice of tinned peach got temporarily stuck in my daughter's throat; now I always cut them in three. Take skin off fruit and mash up as much as possible until he's a little older.

☐ Do not give children chewable pills until they are at least three years old.

☐ Avoid hard smooth food that needs grinding, such as nuts or boiled sweets, until they are over four. Peanuts are particularly dangerous. If one gets stuck in the windpipe or lungs, it not only makes the baby choke, as would any small object, but also the oil in the nut causes a swelling in the surrounding tissues that can induce a type of pneumonia. This applies only to peanuts, which are potentially so dangerous it's worth banning them from the house until the child is older than four.

☐ Never let toddlers throw nuts and catch them in their mouths.

☐ Old dummies that are beginning to perish must be thrown away (see *Baby's bedroom*, page 53).

☐ Encourage calm eating habits. I know it can be difficult to persuade toddlers to sit quietly to eat (their brother or sister making silly faces can be hilariously funny in the middle of lunch), but even talking or laughing with food in the mouth can be dangerous. Even adults can choke in the middle of dinner while laughing at a joke. Encourage children of all ages to take manageable mouthfuls and chew food well.

☐   Some disposable bibs are dangerous: they can be torn up and bits swallowed or inhaled.

(See also *Clothing and wrapping*, below, *Small objects*, page 46 and *Suffocation*, page 48.)

CLOTHING AND WRAPPING

Babies need to be well wrapped and kept at a constant temperature until they are about one month old, after which their bodies become better at regulating themselves. However, even after one month of age you must make sure he doesn't get too hot or cold; he won't be able to let you know if he's feeling comfortable until he's much older.

☐   Never allow your baby to become overheated. Many modern synthetic materials don't allow the normal evaporation of sweat. As this is the major way a baby has of decreasing his temperature, it is wise to check he is not getting too warm in hot weather or a heated room (see *Baby's bedroom*, page 51).

When you bring your baby into a warm room from outside he may still be suitably wrapped for the cold weather and it is important that some clothing or wraps are removed.

☐   Do not allow your baby to get too cold. Babies are very sensitive to cold and can lose heat quickly, even in their cot or pram. Stretch suits, for instance, aren't warm enough on their own when the baby is out of doors, except on hot days.

Babies can lose heat rapidly from their heads so it is important to keep their heads covered in cold weather and to protect them from draughts. Babies can't tell you when they're cold and they don't shiver – the first sign may be irritability.

To check if your baby is comfortable, put your hand under the covers and feel his skin with your hand. If he is too warm, he will feel hot and sweaty and may be thirsty. If he feels rather chilly, then cuddle him to warm him and add some extra clothes or wraps.

☐ Get in the habit of checking clothes (yours and the baby's) for any loose buttons when you dress him. He will soon like to pull at them and if any came off they might be swallowed.

☐ Be careful of very lacy cardigans, shawls or drawstring ribbons that could catch on parts of the pram or high chair and maybe pull tight round his neck.

☐ Watch disposable nappies carefully. They can be pulled apart when wet, so be careful not to leave them within reach when changing the baby. Some children pull nappies apart while wearing them. If yours does this, put a separate pair of plastic pants on top. Take care to store dry nappies out of reach – even these can be pulled apart and stuffed up noses, inhaled or swallowed.

☐ Use only flame-resistant nightwear for toddlers (see *Fire*, page 27).

COT DEATHS OR SUDDEN INFANT DEATH SYNDROME

Deep down I think all parents have a secret fear of this horrendous tragedy happening to their baby. Cot deaths (or sudden unexpected infant deaths) occur between the ages of one week and two years, although ninety per cent occur under the age of eight months. They are, thankfully, extremely rare indeed, but as they are splashed across the newspapers in dramatic headlines whenever they happen, no parent can fail to be aware of them. Just remember that the odds against it happening are at least 500 to 1, and that the vast majority of babies grow up healthy and happy with nothing other than normal care.

Prevention

Many parents ask whether there is anything special that can be done to prevent a cot death. Research by the Foundation for the Study of Infant Deaths shows that cot deaths probably result not from a single cause but from a combination of factors. Until the reasons for these deaths are known it is not possible to make any suggestions except that your baby should be cared for normally.

This normal care should include never ignoring apparently trivial signs or symptoms in your baby. Always ask your family doctor or health visitor if you have any worries. Follow their advice on the best way to feed and look after your baby (see also *Feeding dangers*, page 21). The advice given on page 10 about how to clothe and wrap him and about the temperature of his surroundings may be relevant.

It is obviously sensible to try to protect him from infections but all babies get colds at one time or another. Simply be extra vigilant during these times.

Monitors

Some parents have heard about the special monitors prescribed by doctors that sound an alarm when the baby stops breathing. There is no good evidence as yet to show their use has reduced the incidence of sudden unexpected deaths. Occasionally a doctor may recommend their use for premature babies who have had particular breathing difficulties, babies who have had previous 'near miss' cot deaths (see below), or for siblings of babies who have died.

Apparently life-threatening events ('near miss' cot deaths)

There are rare occasions when babies have been found collapsed, not breathing, pale, limp and lifeless and have, nevertheless, been resuscitated or have started to breathe again on their own. Later examination shows that most of these cases have been caused by various physical problems, such as the start of an infection, but a few of them have no definite subsequent explanation, and these have come to be known as 'apparently life-threatening events' or 'near miss' cot deaths. However, there is as yet no evidence that they are truly in the same category as cot deaths themselves.

As many of these babies have been resuscitated and gone on to grow up perfectly normally, it is obviously important for every parent to know how to resuscitate his or her child (see page 119).

DROWNING

When a baby falls into water he doesn't automatically try to get his head out as an adult would. His first instinct is to try and take a deep breath to yell. Remember that a baby or toddler can drown in very shallow water – even a bucketful.

- [ ] Don't leave buckets full of water lying around. I read in the newspaper only recently of an eighteen-month-old baby who toppled into a bucket of water and drowned.

- [ ] If there is a pond, swimming pool or even a water trough in your garden, either fence it in securely or cover it over. It is horrifying that babies are still drowning in their own gardens.

- [ ] Teach your child not to go too near the water's edge, and never to walk on to ice on a pond.

- [ ] Never let him out of your sight when in the park, countryside or in an unknown garden. There may be unfenced water.

☐ Swimming for very young babies of around three months (so-called 'water babies') is of doubtful value, and there is some concern about its safety – babies may take in too much water and get too cold.

☐ When he's a little older – it's impossible to give a precise age as babies vary so much, but probably well over six months – you can start gently getting him used to the water. Use pools with very warm water and limit sessions to 30 minutes maximum as he can still get cold very easily.

☐ Never force a baby under the water.

☐ The inflatable armbands, rubber rings or swimsuits with polystyrene floats are very useful for giving confidence in the water and having fun, but please remember they are only swimming aids. Never rely on them as life-preservers.

☐ Don't be complacent once your child can swim; water is still very dangerous and he must always be watched.

ELECTRICITY

☐ Never overload your electricity supply. The average house has one ring circuit per floor (100 sq. m/920 sq. ft), and can take on average $7\frac{1}{4}$ kW (30 amps) – more than enough to cope with usual domestic needs. Do not use adaptors if you haven't sufficient sockets – they are prone to breakage and overheating due to high loading and loose connections. Have single sockets converted to doubles or trebles, or have extra sockets wired in. Consult your Electricity Board if in doubt. If you have round-pin sockets or rubber-covered cables, you should seriously consider having the power circuits or whole house rewired, since the wiring may have deteriorated and be a potential hazard. Most Electricity Boards do a free visual check on wiring.

☐ Be aware of sockets, trailing cables and wires, television sets and other dangerous electrical objects.

☐ Never leave a lamp without a bulb in it as it's only too easy for small exploring fingers to be stuck into the empty fitting. If the lamp had been left switched on, it would give a very bad shock. Try to replace spent bulbs immediately, or leave the faulty bulb in position.

☐ Get into the habit of switching everything off after use, but don't pull plugs out when they are still switched on at the socket; this can cause an arc which over a period of time can burn out the contacts in the socket and lessen the effectiveness of the plug. It can also lead to overheating of the plug.

☐ Fit plugs with sleeved pins on as many items as possible; these have insulating 'sleeves' on two of the three pins to prevent shocks from partly pulled-out plugs. From mid-1988 they are the only type shops are allowed, by law, to sell.

☐ Fit the correct size fuses to electrical appliances (always follow the manufacturer's instructions) and make sure they conform to BS 1362.

☐ Electricity Board shops have a free range of very useful leaflets: 'Plugs and fuses', 'Safety in your Home', and 'Garden Electric Safety'.

(See also *Bathroom*, page 63 and *Kitchen*, page 72).

☐ Buy dummy socket covers if you wish, although you don't really need them if you have modern sockets with safety shutters installed. Unfortunately, older sockets without shutters don't fit the covers available and there isn't really a satisfactory way of protecting the old type of socket from prying fingers. You could cover it with insulating tape if you can't afford to rewire with the new shuttered sockets.

Fuses	
3 amp – for most appliances up to 720 watts (W)	**13 amp – for appliances rated over 720 watts (W)**
Radios	Irons Kettles Fan heaters
Table lamps	Electric fires Lawn mowers
Soldering irons	Toasters Deep fat fryers
Televisions*	Refrigerators Freezers
Electric blankets	Washing machines
Audio and hi-fi	Tumble dryers
Slow cookers	Spin dryers
	Vacuum cleaners
*Some TV manufacturers recommend a 5 amp fuse	Dishwashers

The Electricity Council – EC 4740/2.87

☐ Special care should be taken with time-switched heaters – they must always be well clear of furnishings. No heater, time-switched or otherwise, should be covered with drying clothes. Time switches must never be fitted to radiant fires.

☐ Electrocution is a real danger if wires are frayed or broken. Replace flexes on all electrical equipment as soon as they show signs of wear; mending them with insulating tape isn't good enough.

☐ Consider buying a residual current device, which can be used in any 13 amp socket – especially worthwhile when using DIY or gardening equipment. This senses tiny differences in load between live and neutral current: in other

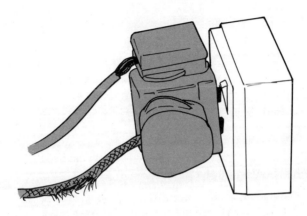

words, when there is more electricity going in than coming out. The residual current device can spot this in a fraction of a second and cuts off the supply before you suffer injury.

☐ Better still, install a residual current device next to your fuse box to protect all your socket outlets. This works on the same principle mentioned above, but reacts to a fault on any socket in the house. Before a residual current device is installed, you must check that your system is earthed properly and that the wiring is safe. This is not a DIY project; you should contact your Electricity Board or a qualified electrician.

FALLS

Falls are the fourth largest cause of accidental death among children in Great Britain.

All babies fall at one time or another – banged heads and bruised knees seem to be an obligatory part of growing up. You certainly won't be able to avoid them completely, but you can try to prevent any bad ones.

The commonest areas of danger are stairs, steps, beds, tables, chairs, changing tables, baths, high chairs, prams, shopping trolleys and tricycles.

☐ Don't leave baby alone on your bed. Remember there will suddenly come a time (from as young as two months) when he starts to roll over, and a fall from even a low bed can be quite a bump for a small baby. We have rushed to hospital in a panic on several occasions and one was from a relatively slight fall off the bed; I was convinced my son had dislocated his shoulder but luckily it was only bruised.

☐ Discourage toddlers from running round in socks without shoes on uncarpeted floors; it makes it far too easy to slip and fall.

☐ Beware of rugs on polished floors. At least put non-slip backings on them.

☐ Watch out for telephone wires and electrical flexes that can easily be tripped over.

☐ Be aware of flimsy pieces of furniture that baby could tip over on to himself when he starts trying to pull himself up by hanging on to things. You won't be able to secure all potential hazards of this kind – even a chair pulled over on to a baby can cause very nasty bumps and bruises – so you will have to watch him carefully at this stage.

(See also *Safety in the Home*, pages 50–82.)

☐ Make sure toddlers' clothes are not long enough to trip them up when they start to walk

☐ Baby-walkers are the single item of child equipment that cause most accidents. They can tip up very easily over small level changes – from floor to rug, or over a threshold – or by the baby leaning over or being pushed by a brother or sister. They also enable the baby to move around extremely fast which can be dangerous at the top of stairs, near front doors

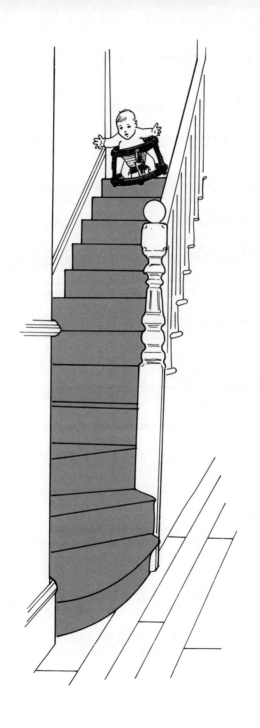

or anywhere they can pull down dangling wires or get near hot stoves and heaters. Some models have dangerous hinges where fingers can get trapped.

If you want to use one you must watch the baby all the time he is in it, keeping its use to smooth flat surfaces well away from obstructions. Buy one that conforms to BS 4648 (among other things this will have a permanent label reading, 'Warning: never leave your baby alone in this walker').

Remember, baby-walkers are not necessary and there is strong evidence, supported by the Chartered Society of Physiotherapy, that they can impair natural foot development and slow down a child's ability to walk. (But my children used one – I hadn't done all this research then!)

☐ Bouncing cradles are useful pieces of equipment, but are a very common cause of falls, particularly when left occupied and unwatched on a table-top or work surface. You must keep your eye on them all the time. Feed baby on the floor rather than take risks; babies never fall off the floor . . .

☐ High chairs should not be used until the baby is at least six months old. Check the safety of the model you buy; some can topple with the wriggling of an active baby, so make sure the

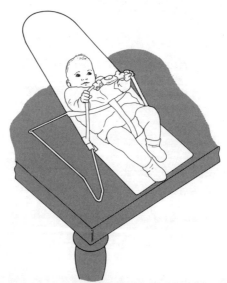

one you choose conforms to BS 5799. Always put the baby in a harness which you keep permanently clipped to the high chair; you don't want to have to search for it when he's screaming for his strained carrots. A harness that conforms to BS 6684 will have been tested for strength and will be made from non-toxic material (in case he prefers it to the carrots).

Be careful with high chairs that clip on to the table – there are some flimsy models about. Choose one that screws on to the table with a clamp, and make sure the table you fix it to is sturdy – it's quite easy for the whole table to tip over with the weight of a toddler. There will be no BS number for this type of chair for a few years yet.

☐ Booster seats can be very dangerous. These are plastic 'boxes' that simply sit on normal chairs, sometimes fastened by a plastic strap. They have no safety harness and no loops to attach one, so a child can easily fall off.

FEEDING DANGERS

It is important to feed your baby correctly and it is generally acknowledged that breast is best. Coughs, colds and tummy upsets are less frequent in breast-fed babies because breast milk helps them to resist and recover from infection.

The early months of breast-feeding are the most valuable and, of course, it's a very special and delightful time for both mother and baby. I look back on my breast-feeding days with much nostalgia. It's also much easier than bottle-feeding if you're basically a lazy person as I am – no mixing, no sterilizing, the supply is always with you and comes ready at the perfect temperature.

If you do decide to bottle-feed, the proprietary baby-milks are so good nowadays that you will almost certainly have no problems at all, but take care to stick to a few basic rules.

☐ It is vital you mix the bottle-feeds exactly as directed. Never be tempted to strengthen the mixture by adding extra milk powder. A doctor tried to explain to me exactly why this is so dangerous but the simplest way I can put it is that the liquid becomes chemically overloaded with minute particles which the baby's system cannot cope with.

☐ Never guess at quantities; measure accurately.

☐ Always use a proper baby-milk preparation until the baby is six months, not ordinary cow's milk or evaporated milk.

☐ Take care to clean and sterilize bottles well – dirty bottles or teats could give your baby an infection. Sterilizing is very easy now; you just buy one of the many sterilizing products at your chemist, make up a fresh solution each day as directed and pop everything into it after washing. The bottle, teat, screw ring and measuring spoon should all be sterilized, and if you use a dummy it's a good idea to put that in the solution as well. I used to express milk so someone else could feed the baby now and then and I found it easy to get in the habit of putting everything in the sterilizing solution.

☐ Always make sure the baby has enough water to drink in hot weather, particularly if he is sweating. Babies aged over one month are sometimes thirsty and want a drink of water (without sugar) which has been boiled once only and cooled. This is especially important if they are feverish or have a cold, a chest infection, diarrhoea or vomiting.

☐ Do not feed solids before the age of three months. Most doctors and health visitors agree that it's better to wait until about four months if you can. I know how tempting it is to start them early. For one thing, if your baby isn't sleeping very well you may fondly imagine that filling him up with something solid is going to help. This is not necessarily so I'm afraid (I know only too well after years of well-fed, wide-awake babies). Some doctors believe starting certain foods too early can even set up allergic reactions. Check with your health visitor about what foods to start your baby on and when.

(See also *Choking*, page 7.)

FINGERS

☐ Fingers can easily get squashed in doors – try to be aware of this when you go to shut a door. This is the kind of danger that a child cannot possibly be aware of, so you must be vigilant for him.

Little fingers are often put in the crack by the hinges; try to teach your child how dangerous this is when he can begin to understand. There is an easy-to-fit, inexpensive device available from baby-care shops which you attach to the top of a door to stop it slamming, but as other houses are very unlikely to have them fitted I think it would be dangerous for the baby to assume all doors are safe. It might be worth fitting one on a particularly heavy, dangerous door that always slams.

☐ It's very easy for a toddler to shut his fingers in a drawer. Try to teach him not to put them inside and try to shut all drawers as soon as you have finished using them.

☐ As with falls, it's only too likely that his fingers will get caught in something eventually and you mustn't feel guilty about it – most incidents are very slight. In any case, fingers can recover from the most amazing crunches without any permanent damage.

(See also *The car*, page 89.)

FIRE

House fires are the commonest cause of accidental death of children in the home. They also cause horrific suffering in non-fatal accidents and the burns inflicted may leave permanent scarring, both mental and physical. It is every parent's duty to protect their child as far as possible from being at risk from fire. Prevention is the key. Do ask your local fire station – they will be delighted to help and their advice is free.

☐ Most fires are caused by smokers. Always extinguish cigarettes properly and empty ashtrays (into a metal rather than a plastic bin).

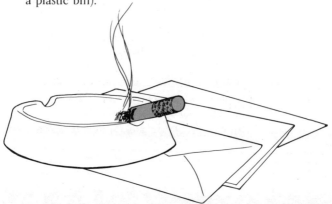

☐ Certain furniture (polyurethane-foam-filled suites with poly-ester covers) and some kinds of bedding burn like tinder if touched with a lighted match or cigarette, frequently causing fatal fires. When polyurethane foam burns, it gives off toxic fumes which contain cyanide. All the children who have recently died in fires were not burnt to death, but died from inhaling poisonous smoke. New government legislation now bars the manufacture of such polyurethane-foam merchan-dise. Please avoid buying potentially lethal items – look for the green safety label which shows that the furniture is resistant to the lighted-match test – and check your old furniture for dangerous materials.

☐ Place a guard around every fire and heater. This is essential. Make sure you get one that has a top as well as sides. BS 6539 has hooks that enable it to be fixed to the wall for added stability, and a fine mesh to prevent children from reaching the fire. For open fires you also need a spark-guard within the ordinary fire-guard – choose BS 3248.

Electric, gas or paraffin heaters must be fitted with guards that conform to BS 1945. Don't rely on the metal bars on the heaters themselves – they can get very hot. A mobile gas cylinder heater must have one of the guards specifically designed for it. A toddler can put fingers through most guards, so make sure he can't touch anything hot once the guard is in place. There are horrifying instances of crawling babies, attracted by the bright red bars, grasping the elements of small electric fires and deforming their hands for life.

☐ Position mobile heaters where they cannot be knocked over or moved while they are still alight.

☐ Make sure all your heaters are safety ones which conform to BS 3456.

☐ Store matches, lighters and inflammable liquids well out of children's reach. In America fires are frequently caused by young children playing cars with disposable stick lighters, running them along the carpet to make them spark.

☐ Unplug/switch off all fires and electrical appliances when not in use. Televisions and videos are quite safe these days, being made to high safety standards, so they do not have to be unplugged.

☐ Close all doors before going to bed.

☐ If you have security devices such as window locks, make sure you keep the keys handy.

☐ Never install totally sealed double glazing; it would prevent you escaping if a fire broke out.

☐ Have an emergency fire-exit plan that everyone in the house understands. Only you know the best way out of your house in the event of a fire. If the windows or back door are kept locked at night for instance, see that the keys are kept in an easily accessible place.

☐ Try to buy flame-resistant nightwear for children. Currently, nightdresses and dressing-gowns must be made from material which does not flare up or burn easily and must comply with BS 5722. At the moment no other sleepwear is regulated in this way.

☐ Fire blankets are very useful in the event of kitchen fires, particularly burning saucepans. A woollen (rather than glass fibre) one is best, but make sure it conforms to BS 6575. It should be about 90 cm/36 in square. Keep it away from the oven, so you won't have to reach over the blaze to get it. (See also page 66.)

☐ Fire extinguishers are not officially recommended for use in the home as they may tempt you to stay and fight the fire rather than getting out. Apart from this, really reliable ones are expensive and small aerosols have limited life and use – only 40 seconds of spray. If you miss your target or dither about you could find yourself in a blazing inferno by having wasted time. For this reason they are not recommended, even for small kitchen fires. They can give a false sense of security.

☐ Paraffin heaters must comply with BS 3300. They will then automatically cut out within 15 seconds if tipped over. They will also have been tested for stability and will not give off smoke, excessive amounts of carbon dioxide or have an unguarded flame.

☐ Smoke detectors are excellent. Some people think that the smell of smoke would wake them up without a detector. It might do, but there again it might not, and smoke can quickly kill. The fire brigade would like to see every home fitted with at least one smoke detector.

There are inexpensive models on the market which sound an alarm on sensing smoke and it is well worth investing in one (or several if you can afford to). To do its job properly a detector needs to be close enough to the fire to respond quickly, but also in a position where its alarm can be heard throughout your home. The alarm must be loud enough to wake you and your family. (Note that a correctly positioned smoke detector is too high to be triggered by cigarette smoke.)

If you can only afford one, install it at the top of the central stairwell (or in the hall in a flat). Smoke rises, so position it high up, if not on the ceiling then on a wall, about 30 cm / 12 in from a door. In an average house, a second detector should be fitted near (not in) the kitchen – preferably outside the kitchen door. If you have a really big house, you can have interlinked smoke detectors which have one central power source.

Smoke detectors can be battery or mains powered. The battery type is cheaper, easier to fit and just as reliable as the mains type, but you must remember to change the battery every year. Some models are self-monitoring and will flash or give a signal when the battery is getting low, but you must check it when you have been away for a few days in case you missed the signal. Whatever type you buy, make sure it conforms to BS 5446 – there are some very cheap foreign detectors which are just not reliable.

There is an excellent booklet called *Smoke Detectors in the Home* available from your local fire brigade; do read it. It gives detailed information on what types to buy and where to position them. Also remember your local fire brigade will be glad to advise you.

(See also *Baby's bedroom*, page 56, *Kitchen*, page 66 and *Sitting room*, page 73.)

HANDLING YOUR BABY

When I got my first baby home I treated her like glass – the first time I took her out in her pram I took my sister with me and we lifted the wheels over all the bad cracks in the pavement because I couldn't bear to think of her being bumped about. By the time I got to my third child I was racing up the street to the supermarket at fifty miles an hour with children bouncing in all directions.

Yes, of course a baby needs gentle, careful handling but they're not as fragile as they may seem to a new parent.

☐ Always support his head until his neck has enough strength for him to do it himself, but if you do let it loll once or twice, don't panic: we've all done it – it won't fall off. By about six weeks he will be able to balance his head upright while whoever is carrying him keeps still. If you walk around carrying him or bend down while you are holding him, you will still need to support his head with your hand to prevent it flopping. By about three months his head will only need supporting if you move him suddenly or pick him up unexpectedly.

☐ When out walking, be careful not to jerk a dawdling toddler suddenly by the arm or swing him roughly when playing. It's only too easy to produce a 'pulled elbow' which can make the arm look paralysed. Although this is not serious it will need to be seen by a doctor.

☐ Teach your baby as young as possible that some objects are forbidden: he won't know at this stage what is dangerous and it's impossible to remove every hazard. If he does grab a forbidden object, take it away matter-of-factly and say 'no'. Distract him immediately with something more interesting: you don't want to start a running battle over every potential danger, but if he does protest stay firm and endure any ensuing tantrum. He's got to learn that you mean it when you say 'no'.

IMMUNIZATION

Please make sure your baby has his immunizations. This is one of the most important things you can do to ensure his future health. During his first two years he will be offered protection against diphtheria, whooping cough, tetanus, polio, measles, mumps and rubella (German measles). Whooping cough vaccine is 80 per cent effective while all the others are virtually 100 per cent.

IMMUNIZATION PROGRAMME

AGE	VACCINE	METHOD
3 to 6 months	Diphtheria Tetanus Whooping cough (pertussis)	By injection
	Polio	By mouth
6 to 8 months	Diphtheria Tetanus Whooping cough	By injection
	Polio	By mouth
10 to 14 months	Diphtheria Tetanus Whooping cough	By injection
	Polio	By mouth
16 to 24 months	Measles Mumps Rubella	By injection
5 years	Diphtheria Tetanus	By injection
	Polio	By mouth

You may have read in the newspapers about problems with the whooping cough vaccine. If you are worried, talk to your health visitor or doctor, but there are very few reasons against giving it to most babies.

☐ Do tell the doctor if your baby is unwell on the day he is due to have his immunization – the doctor might wish to postpone it. If your baby becomes feverish, irritable or develops a high temperature after immunization, let the doctor know.

LEAVING YOUR BABY

You will never want to leave your baby with anyone who is too young or inexperienced to cope in an emergency. There is no legal 'minimum age' for a person left in charge of a baby, but sixteen is the age recommended by the Child Accident Prevention Trust. Babies can be left with older siblings, but there are legal repercussions if there is an accident such as a fire and you've left the fire unguarded. Obviously you must use your common sense – teenagers vary widely in the amount of responsibility they can be expected to take.

There are several things you can do to improve your peace of mind while away from your child.

☐ Try to use someone recommended personally by a friend, or if you have to use an agency, ask for references and check them by telephone. People will often say over the phone what they are reluctant to put in writing.

☐ Whenever possible, leave your babysitter or childminder the telephone number of where you are going (and the address, in case the phone is out of order). Encourage her to use it if she is at all worried. Some friends of mine had an unpleasant experience when they went out to dinner recently. Their young baby was taken ill and the babysitter tried all evening to contact them but their host had taken the phone off the hook so that the evening should not be interrupted by any calls . . . In this case the baby turned out to be fine, but it shows that it's worthwhile checking the telephone is working and that you've given the right number when you arrive at your destination.

☐ Make sure the babysitter can hear the baby: perhaps via a 'baby alarm' (see page 57).

☐ Give your babysitter every detail of baby's feeds and routine. Also tell her if the baby has been unwell or has any particular problems and let her know what to watch out for.

It's a very good idea to write out a card with all the baby's details on it as follows:

ROBERT SMITH
Date of birth: 8/4/88
Home tel. no: 01–432 1234

Father: John Smith   Mother: Jane Smith
Work no: 01–222 2345   Work no: 01–123 4567

DOCTOR:

Dr S. Brown
54 Green Street
London SW2
Tel: 01–223 4321
AFTER 6 P.M. EMERGENCY NO: 01–223 2121

NEAREST ACCIDENT AND EMERGENCY DEPT:
St Honor's
43 Blue Street
London SW1
Tel: 01–444 4321

Robert is allergic to: Peanut butter, Egg, Penicillin

This would be useful not only for the babysitter or childminder (stick it on the wall or near the telephone), but could be put in the baby's changing bag if he is left with a friend for the morning while you go shopping or whatever.

☐ Encourage your sitter to read the emergency section in this book, or leave it in a prominent place, such as near the telephone, and tell her it's there.

☐ Make sure she knows your fire-escape routine.

PETS

Pets can cause problems: some doctors believe that having an animal in the house can set up an allergic reaction in babies or young children, but there's not enough evidence to insist all family pets are thrown out.

Dogs

Dog bites, usually to the limbs or face, are unfortunately remarkably common in young children. In the majority of cases the animal is known to the child. Jealousy is often a cause, so please be aware of this possibility, particularly if you are bringing home a new baby. Peter Neville of the Animal Behaviour Centre recommends the following precautions:

☐ On the first day a new baby is brought home, formally introduce the dog to him, keeping the dog on a lead. Dogs are social animals and accept people as superior. One of the worst things you can do is ban contact entirely. This almost guarantees the dog doing something awful when it finally meets the child.

☐ Never leave a dog alone with a child.

☐ Always favour the baby over the dog in the dog's presence. It is a great mistake to give the dog more affection than the child, even inadvertently.

☐ The real flash-point comes when the baby becomes mobile and can 'invade' the dog's territory and favourite bolt-holes. This is a time to be very watchful.

☐ Don't punish a dog for being 'grumpy' with a child. As long as it moves out of the way and does not attempt to hurt the child, it should actually be praised or rewarded for doing the right thing.

☐ If a dog is very grumpy over a period of time, it's better to muzzle it rather than to deny access to the baby. The Baskerville muzzle is lightweight and available from pet shops and vets.

☐ Once a child is toddling it's a good idea to organize some games with the dog. Command games are best; the adult can throw a ball or stick and the child can call 'fetch', 'stay', 'sit' or 'drop'. This also reinforces the child's superiority over the dog.

☐ The most 'status-conscious' dogs are adolescent males (six to eighteen months old in most breeds). Bitches are usually all right because their mothering instincts make them more receptive to babies.

☐ If you have had a dog as a child-substitute and then become pregnant, you should accustom the dog to receiving less affection from you during your pregnancy. The dog may become badly behaved as a result, but this should be punished by banishing it to another room. After a while the dog will accept and expect affection only when you are willing to give it.

Other animals

☐ Be aware that cats sometimes like to jump into carrycots or cribs to snuggle against a warm baby.

☐ Keep cat-litter trays well away from crawling or toddling children.

☐ It's best not to let a very young child hold a small animal such as a hamster – neither of them will much enjoy it!

☐ Any animal can act unpredictably, however well you think you know its character. Don't let the baby tease the animal or hold food near to it.

☐ Don't let the baby pat an animal when it is eating as the pet may snap.

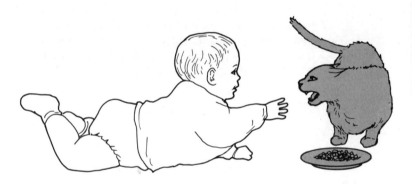

☐ Discourage children from kissing any animal or hugging near its face; the first is certainly unhygienic and the second is potentially dangerous.

(See also *The garden, park or countryside*, page 94.)

POISONING

Be aware of potential poisons such as drugs and medicines, household cleaners, cosmetics and even some household plants. Suspected poisoning is one of the commonest accidents among children aged between one and four. Remember, a baby's ability to discriminate between safe foods and unpleasant-tasting, dangerous substances does not develop until the age of two or three.

Alcohol

☐ Alcohol can be dangerous and a toddler who has drunk a few mouthfuls or more of spirits or fortified wine such as sherry may be seriously affected. Wine is less dangerous because it's less alcoholic, but if in any doubt about the quantity of any alcohol swallowed, seek medical advice. It's hard to believe but one doctor told me that some people think it's a good joke to get a child tipsy at Christmas time. Needless to say he stressed this should never be done.

Drugs and medicines

☐ Never, ever give a baby any kind of pill or medicine without consulting your doctor. If you have any junior aspirin in the house, get rid of it. It is now considered unsuitable for babies and children under twelve, owing to a possible link between aspirin and a rare disease called Reye's Syndrome. If you need a safe painkiller, use a paracetamol-based syrup – but ask your doctor's advice first.

☐ The drugs most commonly taken accidentally by children are:
Cough and cold medicines
Painkillers
Anti-depressants and tranquillizers
Vitamins
Antibiotics
Oral contraceptives

Anti-depressants, tranquillizers and aspirins are the most dangerous. Iron is highly toxic, although less often taken. Oral contraceptives, although not particularly dangerous, are frequently swallowed. I read in the newspaper while writing this book of four very small children who between them swallowed forty-two birth control pills. They suffered no apparent ill effects – although the doctor on duty waggishly remarked that none of them would get pregnant for some time . . .

☐ Always put medicines away after use. Most drug-poisoning accidents happen when recently acquired medicines are left out after use, either in the middle of the night or during the day when you are called to the telephone or otherwise distracted.

☐ Take care that visiting friends or relatives (especially grandparents) do not leave their medicines in accessible places; they may have drugs in their jacket pockets, handbags or bedrooms.

☐ Be careful when the family is under stress. This is often a time when children are ignored and manage to get hold of drugs or medicines. There also may be tranquillizers around the house.

☐ Ask your chemist to supply all the family's drugs and medicines in child-resistant containers. If you find them difficult to open ask the chemist to show you how to do it.

All aspirin and paracetamol sold over the counter or on a hospital prescription must by law be supplied in a child-resistant pack (bottles with special tops or in blister sheets of individually foil wrapped pills). All other prescribed pills – including aspirin and paracetamol on a GP's prescription – are supplied in child-resistant packs only by voluntary agreement.

Do remember these containers are only *resistant* – children as young as two have been known to open them, so you must still keep the containers in a safe place. (I found a bottle of pills in the toybox the other day! I don't know how they got there, but you can imagine how guilty I felt, especially as I was working on this book at the time . . .)

For some time the official advice printed on medicine labels has been 'Keep out of the reach of children'. Recent surveys revealed that people had been following the advice very well, but that the number of suspected poisonings had not decreased by as much as expected. The labels may now be changed to: 'Keep out of the reach *and sight* of children' – two-year-olds are very good climbers . . .

☐ Never decant drugs into containers which don't close securely, especially containers that are associated with food and drink.

☐ Try not to keep drugs in handbags: they hold a particular fascination for toddlers.

☐ Try not to take pills in front of children – they may imitate you later.

☐ Get rid of all old drugs and medicines and keep current ones safely locked away.

☐ Teach your child the dangers of pills as soon as he is old enough to understand. If you give him vitamins, make it quite clear that they are not sweets and that he must only have one.

☐ Don't let anyone else give him any pills of any kind; explain to him that he mustn't accept them from anyone but his parents.

Storing drugs and medicines

A childproof cabinet with a no-key medicines area is a sensible investment. Ask your retailer to get you one if he doesn't stock them; the more we all demand these things, the more they will become available to as many families as possible. Lockable cabinets are next best and there is a wide variety available. Be sure to keep the key handy (but not on top or next to the cabinet). If you prefer, fit a cupboard that sits flush with the wall and looks like a mirror. These have a discreet, spring-loaded mechanism in one corner which must be pushed quite hard to open the mirror door. As they don't look like cupboards, children can remain blissfully unaware of their dangerous contents.

Alternatively, fit childproof catches to your existing medicine cabinet. They work for most children up to about three and are fairly easy to fit. They are inexpensive and available from most department stores and baby shops. As an interim measure, you could keep your drugs in a lockable drawer.

The kitchen is considered a good place to store medicines. It sounds surprising, but the Child Accident Prevention Trust recommends it as an alternative to the bathroom, where the child is more likely to be alone. People also tend to be more reliable about putting medicines away if they are kept in the kitchen.

☐ If you do keep any medicines in the kitchen, make sure they are safely locked away, out of reach and out of sight. Be extra careful if you have to keep any in the fridge, as these can easily be taken when you're not looking and are likely to be mistaken for food or drink. Ask your pharmacist if it's really necessary to keep them in the fridge; quite often a reasonably cool place will do instead.

(See also *Baby's bedroom*, page 58; *Other bedrooms*, page 58; *Bathroom*, page 61.)

Newsprint

☐ In some circumstances newsprint can be toxic. Printing inks, particularly coloured inks used in magazines, have been known to contain lead. However, there are no recorded cases of children eating vast amounts of newspaper so the likelihood of lead-poisoning from this source is slight. Even so, it is reassuring to note that many of the large ink manufacturers are trying to remove the lead from their products.

Tobacco

☐ Cigarettes and cigarette ends can be extremely toxic if eaten. However, nicotine is not particularly well absorbed and as it causes prompt vomiting is rarely fatal. If your child has eaten one whole cigarette or three cigarette ends, this is potentially dangerous. Symptoms generally appear within 30 to 60 minutes and include vomiting, sweating, pallor, increased salivation, dizziness and drowsiness. Consult your doctor immediately and in future keep cigarettes, smoked and unsmoked, well away from babies and toddlers.

Household and garden poisons

It is impossible to list any 'safe' or 'dangerous' cleaning materials, cosmetics or gardening products as there are so very many on the market and you can never be sure what they contain. It is best to assume they are all potentially harmful. Remember aerosols can be sprayed in the eyes, at worst causing blindness. (See also *Bathroom*, page 62, *Kitchen*, page 67 and *The garden, park or countryside*, page 94.)

☐ Watch out for 'attractively' coloured liquids. There is an amber disinfectant that looks horribly like orange squash, for instance, and another in a tempting floral package.

☐ Never transfer cleaners into soft-drink bottles. Try to buy them in child-resistant containers which are now becoming available. (Many household chemicals are now obliged by law to be sold in such containers.) You could even buy an empty childproof container and transfer any dangerous cleaning products you feel may be in constant use.

☐ Keep household cleaners, such as bleach, polishes, detergents and disinfectant, out of reach and out of sight, ideally in locked cupboards or on high shelves.

☐ Don't ever give a bottle that has contained a household poison to a child to play with, even if it has been rinsed out. It may contain tiny amounts of the product which could be swallowed or poured into the eyes.

☐ Sterilizing tablets can easily be swallowed and cause internal burns; keep them well out of reach.

☐ Keep the most dangerous chemicals – paint strippers, weed killers and so on – out of the house, preferably safely locked away in a shed or garage.

☐ Don't leave chemicals lying around while you're using them, particularly while cleaning or decorating. A jam-jar of white spirit with a brush soaking in it can be picked up and drunk in a split second. Explain to the baby once he is old enough to understand that he must never drink anything unless he has been given it by an adult.

☐ If you have old, painted furniture that may be chewed at or licked by the baby, bear in mind that it may contain lead, which is poisonous. If in doubt, re-paint with safe, modern paint.

Houseplants

Most houseplants are non-toxic, and there are no reported deaths from houseplant poisoning, but it's obviously sensible to teach your baby not to eat any leaves or flowers (a rubber plant doesn't look very elegant with bites out of it in any case). Many retailers now give details on the plant labels of any possible poisonous effects. In all suspected cases of poisoning from plants, take a sample of the plant with you to the hospital to aid identification and help in the choice of treatment. The following illustrations show some houseplants which can have toxic effects if eaten.

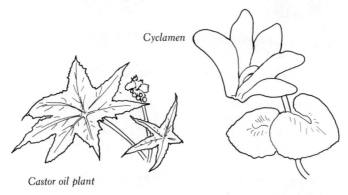

Cyclamen

Castor oil plant

Castor oil plant (*Ricinus communis*), June–October. Mildly toxic leaves. Children are particularly attracted to the creamy purple beans which, if chewed, are highly poisonous; even one bean can be fatal. If unchewed, the beans pass harmlessly through the system as the hard bean coating prevents release of the toxin. Symptoms can take from several hours to a few days to appear. Note that the plant can cause severe allergic reactions in hypersensitive individuals.
Cyclamen (*Cyclamen* spp.). The bulbs are particularly toxic, but the stems and leaves can also cause stomach upsets when eaten.

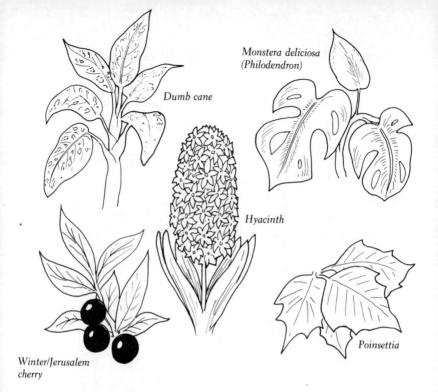

Dumb cane

Monstera deliciosa
(Philodendron)

Hyacinth

Winter/Jerusalem
cherry

Poinsettia

Dumb cane (*Dieffenbachia sequine*). The sap is poisonous and causes immediate and painful burning and swelling of the mouth and tongue, sometimes leading to breathing and speech difficulties. It may also cause blistering of the skin if handled. Symptoms can last from 4 to 48 hours.

Hyacinth (*Hyacinthus* spp.). Children may be tempted to nibble these pretty and highly perfumed flowers, but only the bulb is really toxic. It can cause stomach upset and diarrhoea if eaten. Note that handling the plant may cause mild skin irritation.

Philodendron (*Philodendron* spp.). Breaking the leaves or stems of this plant causes the release of a white, sticky sap which causes immediate painful burning in the mouth if eaten. Symptoms include excessive salivation, swelling of the mouth, stomach pains and diarrhoea.

Poinsettia (*Poinsettia pulcherrima*). This pretty seasonal plant, with bright red leaves resembling flowers, is very attractive to children. The bitter sap is irritant, affecting the skin if touched; the sap or any part of the plant can cause gastric upsets if eaten.

Winter/Jerusalem cherry (*Solanum capsicastrum/ pseudo-capsicastrum*). These popular Christmas plants have large, round, bright-orange berries, which are more poisonous when green and unripe. However, more than 2 or 3 ripe berries may cause stomach upsets and sweating if eaten.

SCALDS

Hot drinks are a common cause of scalding – the largest cause of serious non-fatal accidents to children under five.

☐ Tea and coffee are particularly dangerous. A baby's arm can reach out in a split second and grab a pot or cup and a hot drink can scald up to 30 minutes after it has been poured. Please never underestimate the horrendous suffering that can be caused by such a common, simple accident. (See also *Kitchen*, page 68 and *Other bedrooms*, page 58.)

☐ A tray of hot drinks on the bed can be dangerous with young children around – one bounce and it can tip over. We thought our children were well past that particular danger and recently put our morning tea on the bed. Unfortunately Superman took a flying leap at his brother and missed, sending the tea everywhere and scalding his foot. It was heartbreaking to see Superman crying because his foot hurt and we now keep all hot drinks well out of superheroes' reach.

☐ Hot water in baths, sinks and basins can also scald. Ideally you should turn down the thermostat on your boiler to 50 °C/ 120 °F and you will protect the baby from painful scalding. It is a simple measure which, if taken in all households with young babies, would save vast amounts of suffering. You may feel it would stop the rest of the family having the boiling hot baths they enjoy, but it could be worth trying for a while to achieve peace of mind. (See also *Kitchen*, page 64, and *Bathroom*, page 61.)

SMALL OBJECTS

Bits and pieces left lying around may be picked up and swallowed, inhaled, pushed up noses or into ears. Get into the habit of picking up anything that is dropped, paying particular attention to coins, buttons, beads and bits of toys. Also try to keep dangerous objects out of reach: remember a crawling baby can extend his height by another 60 cm/2 ft by pulling himself up. Everything within about 90 cm/3 ft of the floor is within reach.

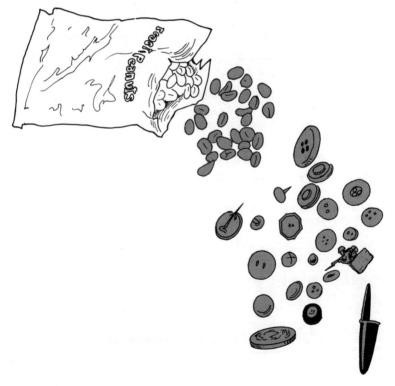

☐ Common causes of choking include deflated balloons, chewable pills, egg shell, baby powder and tops off drink cans. Don't let the baby play with anything small enough to be swallowed, especially something round like a marble.

☐ Coins should not be given to young children as a reward.

☐ Pen-tops are sometimes inhaled by young children.

☐ Button batteries from small computer games and musical birthday cards sometimes contain mercury which can leak if swallowed. Others may cause corrosive burns.

☐ Plastic fastenings from packets of bread can also be dangerous if swallowed.

☐ Pencils and pens are frequently chewed by toddlers: bits may come off and cause choking.

☐ Teach toddlers not to run around with anything in their mouths, especially dangerous sharp objects like pencils. If they fall they can suffer severe injury. Even copying a brother or sister by putting a recorder or penny whistle in the mouth can hurt the back of the throat if they trip.

☐ Rubber bands are a temptation to toddlers. They sometimes wind them round their fingers and leave them there all night. This can stop the circulation and result in damage to the fingertips.

(See also *Other bedrooms*, page 58 and *Toys*, page 48.)

SMOKING

Apart from the vastly increased danger of fire from cigarettes, matches and lighters, it is also worth mentioning that babies in houses where one or more parents smoke tend to get more respiratory infections than in non-smoking households. The incidence of such infections increases according to the number of smokers in the house and occurs particularly in the first two years of life.

Lung growth tends to be less than expected, and the baby may be wheezier than normal in his first year. In a recent study commissioned by the government, Sir Peter Froggatt of Belfast University reported that passive smokers within families also have a greatly increased risk of developing lung cancer.

Remember – children learn by example; if you are a non-smoker, your children are less likely to be smokers when they grow up. So if you needed yet another good reason to give up . . .

SUFFOCATION

☐ Plastic bags and clingfilm are very dangerous – never leave them lying around and keep them well out of reach.

☐ Remove any plastic covering from a new purchase immediately and throw it away.

☐ Tear up and throw away plastic bags or keep them locked away.

(See also *Choking*, page 7, *Clothing and wrapping*, page 11 and *Baby's bedroom*, page 51.)

TOYS

All toys sold in Great Britain should ideally comply with BS 5665 or BS 3443, but manufacturers are not legally obliged to ensure this. Toys must be large enough not to be swallowed, and not have any small parts that may come off. Plastic doesn't show on X-rays, so it can be very difficult if small plastic parts are swallowed. Don't assume toy manufacturers – even so-called 'safety-conscious' ones – make only safe toys. The narrowest part of any toy should be 10–13 cm/4–5 in wide to avoid going right in the mouth.

☐ Older children's toys should not be used by younger ones.

☐ Some cheap, unsafe toys are available, particularly around Christmas time. Although they are clearly intended for very young children, the manufacturers get round the law by labelling them as only for older children. Examine such toys carefully before buying.

☐ Strings on toys must be no longer than 30 cm/12 in because of the danger of strangulation.

Batteries have been known to leak in certain toys and cause acid burns. In order to prevent such a horrible accident happening to your child, there are several precautions you can take:

☐ Always fit batteries correctly, ensuring that the plus and minus signs match.

☐ As soon as toys show signs of not working properly, replace *all* the batteries at the same time.

☐ Never mix types or makes of battery; the capacity of similar-sized batteries can vary, depending on the manufacturer. Mismatched batteries can cause charging or short-circuiting, possibly leading to leakage and, in certain cases, even fire or explosion.

☐ Battery manufacturers do not consider removing batteries from equipment not in use to be a real safety precaution. If the batteries are old or mismatched, charging will still occur when the batteries are replaced and the equipment is in use.

☐ Never let your baby play with batteries or the battery compartment of toys.

The BBMA (British Battery Manufacturers' Association) produces a free leaflet called *Battery Safety Guidelines*, which contains detailed advice about the use, storage and disposal of batteries (see page 170 for address).

SAFETY IN THE HOME

You will never make your house accident proof, but there are many disasters that can be prevented with a little care and forethought. Try looking at the house from your baby's viewpoint – literally, by getting down on your hands and knees. It will give you a good idea of dangers that would be missed from an adult height.

Don't be depressed if you have to spoil some of your careful decorative planning by moving ornaments, putting a non-slip rug on your polished floor or keeping an unattractive fireguard permanently in your sitting room. Remember that the safety and health of your baby is the most important thing in your life now: if anything happened to him nothing else would matter. In any case the changes will mostly be temporary – the baby will grow into relatively safe adulthood only too soon.

The simplest and most effective safety rule is to try always to be aware of where the baby is. Once he starts crawling he will move surprisingly fast, and you don't want to realize with a lurch of the stomach that you haven't seen or heard him for five minutes. The baby is safest when you are watching him, so you must try and arrange your life in the house so that he is in the same room as you, unless he is safely in the cot or playpen.

BABY'S BEDROOM

This is likely to be the only room in which you will leave the baby alone for relatively long periods, so you must try and see there is no way he can harm himself when you're not watching.

Sleeping arrangements for under-twos

When you first bring the baby home you will want to keep him in something fairly small so he feels snug and secure. There's no need to spend a fortune on a fancy crib.

▥ Baby baskets are useful for carrying babies around but if you are using one for night-time sleeping, do check that it's stable and that the lining is well stitched down.

▥ Baby nests are only for carrying baby around: don't leave him to sleep in one. If the baby gets too hot or is unwell then sweat or vomit can make the material impermeable and make it hard for him to breathe. Those made to BS 6595 make suffocation as unlikely as possible. If you want to have one for carrying him around, try to buy the kind with a long zip down the back; unzip it and open up the bag completely once he is asleep.

▥ A carry-cot is not only fine for sleeping, but also will be useful for transporting him if you buy wheels to go with it – but make sure they fit correctly. Look for BS 3881. It should have handles to allow two people to carry it safely, be secure and be made of non-toxic materials. If buying secondhand, check that the lining is tight and not hanging in loose folds or perished.

▥ Don't use a quilted sleeping bag as the baby can snuggle down too far and suffocate.

▥ The popular 'sleep-sacks' can also be dangerous if they come up high around baby's head; it's very easy to slip down inside them. Only buy the type with shoulder straps: they are just as effective at keeping baby's body and legs cosily tucked in without being dangerous.

▥ When the baby is a little bigger, you will want to move him to a cot. Look for BS 1753 on the label. There have been horrific cases of babies getting their heads trapped between wrongly spaced bars. They should be no less than 25 mm/1 in and not more than 60 mm/2½ in apart.

If the cot has metal guidebars, make sure they are screwed right down, otherwise the baby's clothes can get caught on them.

▥ The most important safety factor of all in a cot is that the mattress fits correctly. It is essential there is no gap between the cot and mattress where the baby's head could get stuck – there must be no space of more than 40 mm/1½ in. Watch for this particularly when buying a secondhand cot. If you do need to buy a new mattress for an old cot, examine the cot thoroughly as they often have the correct mattress size marked on them. A new cot will be clearly labelled to show which size mattress is needed. The mattress should conform to BS 1877.

There is no evidence that the 'safety' mattresses which have airholes under baby's head are any safer than ordinary mattresses. They may reassure parents (I had one for our first baby) but there really is no advantage to them. That also goes for the new 'safety' sheets which have perforations to fit over the 'holey' parts of the mattress!

Bedding

▥ Don't use a pillow – it is unnecessary and dangerous for children under one year. If you want to use one when your child is older, make sure it conforms to BS 1877.

▓ Make sure the bottom sheet fits correctly; it's possible to get tangled in a loose sheet. There should be no folds or baggy bits. The stretchy ones that fit right over are excellent.

▓ Most top covers arc fine as long as they are reasonably loose. A baby will be safe covered with a continental quilt (BS 5335) or sheet and blankets, whichever you prefer.

Cot safety

▓ If he's very active, buy some 'cot-bumpers' to save him banging his head against the bars. (If in doubt, buy them anyway: your docile little darling could turn into an all-in wrestler before you know it.) Do check the length of the ties – they should be no longer than 12 in/30 cm. A baby was tragically strangled recently by the ties of his cot bumpers. I suggest that you check that the ties are firmly attached to the bumper and after knotting them securely, cut them very short.

▓ If your cot has two positions for the base, be sure to lower it as soon as you see signs of the baby starting to clamber about. This is to prevent his climbing out and falling; a fall from the top of a cot rail can be surprisingly bad.

▓ A dummy on a long ribbon can cause strangulation, so tie it to the cot side or a button on your baby's cardigan, leaving a short length of ribbon. Don't use a dummy for too long as eventually the material will perish and lumps may come off and choke the baby. Check it regularly and sterilize in the same way as feeding bottles. Don't ever be tempted to improvise a dummy from a bottle teat or use the dummies which have a container for fruit juice or syrup; choking is a real danger from both. Dummies must conform to BS 5239.

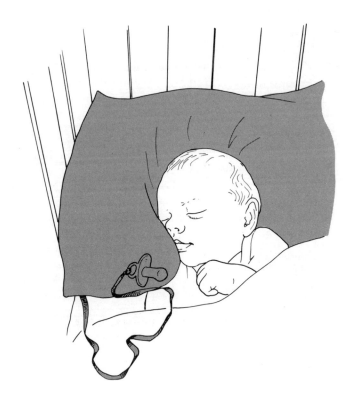

▦ Toys must not be strung across the cot unless they're specifically designed for such a purpose and conform to safety
standards (BS 5665 or BS 3443). Make sure any mobiles
hanging above the cot are secure and will not come down. A
friend heard her baby screaming in the middle of the night
and discovered him tangled in the mobile that had been
hanging over the cot. He was fine but could have done
himself a lot of damage. If you use the type of mobile that is
suspended from a plastic arm ending in a hook, you might

wish to remove the arm and hook at night as well as the mobile: a mother I know hooked her baby in the eye as she lifted him out one night.

▦ When he reaches climbing age, don't put large toys in the cot as he can use them as a ladder. Try to have something soft on the floor under the cot just in case he should ever climb out and fall; he may well suddenly surprise you by his mountaineering ability.

▦ Put baby on his side or tummy when he is going to sleep, placing a rolled up nappy behind his back if necessary to prevent him turning on to his back. Then if he does vomit or bring up a little milk it will drain harmlessly away and not choke him.

▦ Never leave the baby alone in the cot when feeding. A baby left with a propped-up bottle or a rusk can easily choke.

Sleeping arrangements for over-twos

When the baby gets bigger, please think very carefully before moving him into a bed: babies can fall out of bed very easily. It's impossible to give an age guideline as children vary so much in their mobility, but if an under-two is regularly attempting to climb out of the cot, it's probably wise to move him: better to fall from a low bed than over the side of a cot.

If he's not the athletic type you may be able to leave him in the cot even up to the age of two or three. (It has the added advantage of dissuading little visitors from wandering into your bedroom in the middle of the night!)

▦ When you do move your child into a bed, push it against the wall and buy a guard rail (or push up a piece of furniture) for the unprotected side.

Bunks

▐ Choose your bunk beds carefully. Some have highly dangerous, badly spaced guard rails through which a toddler can squeeze and be left hanging by his head. The type with a solid guard instead of a rail is far more satisfactory.

▐ Don't put a child under six in a top bunk.

Heating a baby's room

Keep a young baby's room at an even temperature of about 19 °C / 65 °F, both day and night. It may be worth buying an inexpensive wall thermometer to reassure you. In cold weather newborn babies can lose heat quickly, even in the cot. To check whether he is warm enough put your hand beneath the covers to feel his body. As a general guideline, after the first couple of months the amount of clothing and wrapping for a baby can be best judged by what an adult would feel comfortable in under similar temperature conditions.

▐ Only use a safety heater in baby's room and use a securely fixed guard around it (see *Fire*, page 25).

▐ Have a good look at the room to see if there is anything that could possibly catch fire. Are there any curtains hanging near heaters? A friend of mine in Canada had a terrible accident with her baby when the curtains caught fire from a heater, fell down on to the cot and set it alight. I know it's frightening even to think of it, but if we become aware of these possibilities we're more likely to prevent them.

Equipment

▦ Changing table. There are no safety standards applying to changing tables, but if you want one, try to go for the sturdiest and check it regularly. Never leave the baby alone on a changing table; don't even turn your back for a few seconds. There are many falls from changing tables. If in doubt, change the baby on the floor – babies never fall off the floor.

▦ Make sure any lotions, sterilizing tablets and creams you may need are kept well out of reach of baby and toddler, but near enough so you don't have to leave the baby to fetch them. A high shelf or cupboard nearby is a good idea.

▦ Talcum powder can be easily inhaled and cause bronchitis. Keep it well out of reach when changing nappies.

▦ Check windows for safety. If in any doubt, fit window locks which screw to the frame and allow the window to be opened only a few inches. These are better than vertical bars because if you keep the key handy, the window can still be used as an escape route in a fire.

▦ Don't put any furniture under the window that the baby can climb on to as he gets bigger.

▦ Unless his room is well within earshot, do think about buying a 'baby alarm' – a kind of intercom with a microphone one end so you can always hear the baby. This can be very reassuring, especially at night: if the baby vomited and started to choke and you were unaware of it it could be dangerous. (In any case I'm sure you wouldn't want him to be crying his heart out without your knowing it.)

There are various types of baby alarm – mostly battery operated – and they are available from electrical dealers, large chemists and babycare shops. There is another kind where you simply plug one half of the intercom into an ordinary electrical socket near the baby and the other half into a socket in whatever room you happen to be. However, this type of alarm will only work if used in rooms which are on the same electrical circuit. (Some houses have one circuit per floor, so if the baby was upstairs and you were downstairs, this sort of alarm wouldn't work; it didn't work in our house.)

▚ If the baby has been prescribed any medicine, or is taking paracetamol for pain or feverishness, don't leave it in his room – he may try to take it when you're not there.

OTHER BEDROOMS

Don't confine all your safety precautions to the baby's room. Once toddling, the baby will enter the notorious 'into everything' stage, so be prepared!

▚ Try not to leave cosmetics such as nail-polish remover, nail polish, cologne and hairspray lying on top of the dressing table where a toddler might reach them.

▚ Make sure all drugs and medicines are kept in a safe place, *not* next to the bed or on the dressing table. Remember iron pills are particularly dangerous and care should be taken not to leave them lying around after the birth of your baby or during current pregnancies. Be extra careful of guest bedrooms, particularly a grandparent's. Doctors had trouble helping one little girl who was poisoned when it was found she had had access to twenty-six bottles of her grandfather's pills.

▚ Heated hairstyling brushes and wands may have button batteries in the tops; toddlers have been known to swallow them.

▚ Remember the horrifying danger of hot drinks. Watch that

early morning tea carefully, especially if you're as dozy in the morning as I am.

▦ Older siblings' rooms may contain dangerous toys, unsecured windows, chemistry sets or sharp tools. You can't expect an older child to take responsibility for keeping it safe, so when you're not watching the baby the room must be kept locked or have a gate over the door.

BATHROOM

Baths

An adult bath is not satisfactory for a little baby: buy a small baby bath if you wish, or use the basin.

▓ If you use a bath and stand, make sure it is sturdy and secure.

▓ When the baby has outgrown the baby bath and you move him to the big bath, teach him not to stand up: he can easily slip and hurt himself. Use a rubber mat in the bath.

▓ Water is enormous fun for babies and toddlers, but potentially very dangerous. A baby or toddler can drown in very

shallow water. Never leave your child alone in the bath for even a second. If the doorbell or telephone rings, either ignore it or take the baby with you. If you can't bear to leave the phone unanswered, take it off the hook (or switch on the answering machine if you have one).

Always put cold water in first when running baby's bath, then feel it yourself before you put him in. It should be warm, but not as hot as you would have it for yourself; babies can be scalded in surprisingly low temperatures. The traditional way to test the temperature is to feel it with your elbow, but I've always found that impossible; perhaps I have especially insensitive elbows . . . anyway, you can soon get to know the best way of judging it – I just swish my hand around a bit and when it's a little cooler than I would like it, that's about right. The ideal temperature for a baby's bath is said to be 36–8 °C/97–100 °F, so you could always buy a thermometer if you're unsure. Sometimes with a first baby these little things can make you quite nervous.

After running hot water into a bath or sink from a mixer tap, run cold again so if the baby touches the tap he is not burned.

Don't use the so-called 'support rings' to sit your baby in when he's in the bath – they are not safe.

Bathroom cabinet

Ask your local retailer for a childproof bathroom cabinet or fit child-safety locks yourself (see page 40). You might consider keeping the drugs in the kitchen if there is a lockable cupboard there.

Get into the habit of always putting away pills, medicines, creams and antiseptics. It's all too easy to leave a bottle of pills out by mistake, particularly in the middle of the night: a toddler may wake up earlier than you and find them. Our dog once ate a whole plastic bottle of asthma pills. She spent a couple of days being very unwell, and then fully recovered, but you can imagine how guilty we felt and what a lesson it taught us.

▓ Remember not to leave a razor or used blades lying on the side of the basin. Put used blades into the slot on the back of the box or dispose of them very safely.

▓ Keep hair-remover, bubble bath, shaving cream and other bathroom products well out of reach.

▓ Don't leave bleach or lavatory cleaner on the floor. Keep them in a safe place, preferably locked up or on a high shelf.

▦ Don't use bleach and lavatory cleaner together – the combination gives off dangerous fumes.

▦ Electrical equipment such as portable televisions, hairdryers and fan heaters, should *never* be used in the bathroom. Apart from the risk of dropping them into a bath or a sink of water, which is fatal to someone in the bath, the body is particularly sensitive to electric shock when wet.

▦ Tiled floors can become like skating rinks when wet. Use non-slip bath mats and watch out for sharp edges on baths and showers. As elsewhere in the house, you could tape bubble-pack or cardboard around the corners.

▦ Heated towel rails can give a nasty burn; turn them off or down.

▦ Make sure the locks on your bathroom and lavatory are out of reach of a toddler or are the kind that open from the outside with a coin. In any case, it's wise to teach your child never to lock any door.

▦ A toddler can drown in the lavatory bowl. If there is a danger of your child wandering into the lavatory on his own, there is a device you can fit to the lid which makes it very difficult to open. (It would also save your watch or other interesting objects being thrown into the lavatory to see if they float . . .)

KITCHEN

This is a place to be especially vigilant. When you're cooking or washing up, it's all too easy to become engrossed in what you're doing. Try always to be aware of your baby or toddler as it's impossible to remove all sources of danger.

▥ Try to arrange your kitchen so that you can see your baby while you're at the sink, ironing board or worktop. I have a large mirror stuck on the wall above the taps which is very useful for keeping an eye on the children playing behind me.

▥ Burns and scalds from ovens and hobs are distressingly common, but most of them are avoidable. My children always seemed to want to play right at my feet, where the danger of splashes of hot fat or boiling water was at its greatest. Hob guards are available from babycare shops and

department stores. There are three-sided ones for free-standing cookers or four-sided for hobs set into the worktop, but none of them are really satisfactory. They do prevent saucepans being pulled completely off cooker tops but the guards themselves can get hot.

An Aga or Raeburn gets very hot indeed – not just the hot plates and doors but the entire stove. Fix up a guard to keep the baby right away from it and teach him as early as possible to be aware of the danger.

Some oven doors open downwards, and there have been accidents from children standing on the open door and causing the entire oven to tip forwards. When your baby begins to pull himself up – and that may happen quite suddenly – be aware of the possibility of his touching the hot edge of the hob, or even the rings themselves.

Turn saucepan handles towards the back of the stove, and where possible use the rear rings for most of your cooking.

Make sure nothing inflammable such as curtains or tea-towels hang near enough the hob to be a fire hazard. Don't dry tea-towels on the eye-level grill. (Yes, apparently some people do . . .)

Watch oil or fat on the cooker closely and don't fill saucepans too full of oil – chip-pan fires are very common. Keep a fire blanket (BS 6575) in the kitchen; this is the best way of quickly putting out any burning saucepan. (See also *Fire*, page 27.)

Best of all, make the entire area around the oven and hob forbidden from the word go, and stick to it. A few stern 'no's' early on could prevent later disaster. It's sometimes very difficult to withstand a toddler's temper tantrums and tempting to give in when you're trying to be firm about something, but it really does pay off if you remain adamant about these dangerous things. One parent I know made a safe 'play area' for her child with his own toy cooking utensils. As her floor was tiled, she padded it with an inexpensive rug. The baby could be near to her and entertained, but safe.

▦ You could use a safety gate or barrier to keep the baby out of the dangerous area if he's too young (or stubborn!) to stay away voluntarily (see *Stairs and hallways,* page 75).

▦ Playpens can be very useful. Even if your baby won't stay happily in it for long (none of mine would), it's a safe place to put him down if the doorbell rings, the phone goes or something is boiling over on the stove. Far better to leave him there angrily screaming for a few seconds than let him crawl into danger while your back is turned. Make sure the one you have conforms to BS 4863. If you buy a secondhand one, check that it is sturdy, with rails and lining intact.

▦ The cupboard under the sink is commonly used for storing cleaning materials, but it is not the safest place if you have an inquisitive toddler. Try to store them out of reach, preferably on high shelves.

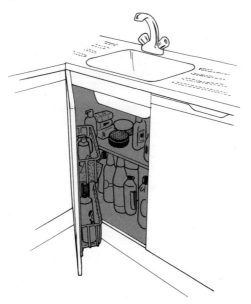

Serving food and drink

▓ Be very careful if you use a microwave oven for warming baby's milk – the liquid can become dangerously hot while the bottle feels cool. Many scalds of mouth and throat have occurred from microwaved food and drink.

▓ Check the temperature of baby's solid food by tasting it yourself before feeding him. He'll need it slightly cooler than is comfortable for you.

▓ Plates and serving dishes can burn when straight from the oven; make sure they're put safely out of reach as you take them out.

▓ Do not pass hot drinks over baby's head, or have a hot drink with a child on your knee. Take care not to leave a cup or teapot full of hot liquid near the edge of the table, or on a low table. This cannot be stressed enough – many babies suffer pain and scarring every year after being scalded by hot tea or coffee. Hot drinks can still scald up to half an hour after they are made.

▓ Don't put a hot drink in front of a young child and expect him to wait until it's cool. Very recently I took my children to the swimming baths and was surprised to see a young mother frantically undressing her screaming toddler in the cafeteria overlooking the pool. I suddenly realized he had been burnt (we rushed him to the lavatory and splashed him with cold water and his injuries luckily proved to be not too serious). His mother explained that the baby's older brother had spilt some of his hot chocolate and as the mother turned to get a cloth she told the younger one not to try to drink his as it was too hot. Unfortunately he paid no attention, tried to drink it and spilt it all over himself.

▓ Tablecloths that the baby can pull at are not a good idea. (I'll never forget the time my brother, then aged twelve, tried to do the magician's trick of pulling the cloth from under a laid

table. There wasn't anything hot on it luckily, but the breakage and mess were quite impressive.) Table mats are just as effective at protecting the table and much safer. Alternatively, use a plastic cloth and pin it to the table.

Kitchen appliances and utensils

▦ If you have a dishwasher, don't leave it open – the cleaning powder is caustic to touch and there may be sharp knives standing upright in the basket which can be extremely dangerous.

▦ Don't assume your food processor is safe just because you have to put the lid on to make it work. The young son of a friend of mine stuck his finger down into the switch and managed to turn it on, severing the top of his finger (which was successfully stitched back on).

▦ Very occasionally toddlers have been known to climb into chest freezers and pull them shut. The danger is that not only are the doors of freezers and fridges hard to open, but also they seal shut excluding all air. Fit childproof locks (see page 40) to prevent this happening.

▦ Switch off the iron as soon as you've finished using it and put it right out of reach. Don't be tempted to leave it on the board, even to answer the telephone or doorbell; the hanging flex makes it dangerously easy to pull down. Wall-mounted

holders can be a good idea. You may be able to fix a coiled flex to your iron, which would make it *far* safer. Ask your local electrical shop.

- Keep the iron out of reach even when it's cold; they are very heavy and can cause injury if dropped.

- Make sure your ironing board is stable.

- If the iron rest is made of asbestos, it must be replaced if it is crumbling or gets wet.

- Keep sharp knives, scissors and other dangerous utensils such as food-processor blades safely out of reach in a childproof drawer.

- Be aware when you have a sharp knife in your hand; it's all too easy to put it down somewhere within baby's reach if the phone rings, or even rush to a screaming child with it still in your hand!

- Tumble driers can be a boon if you're constantly washing baby clothes, but metal snaps on stretch baby suits can become very hot after tumble-drying. Make sure they are cool before dressing baby.

- Washing machines and spin driers can be dangerous. Although they are now made to high safety standards, there is still a danger of children being trapped – perhaps crawling in head first and getting stuck. Older models which can be opened while still spinning can do nasty damage to fingers and even break bones. Keep babies and toddlers well away from them.

- Don't let your toddler get anywhere near the sink if you have an electric waste-disposal unit; they have powerful blades and can be dangerous. If you are thinking of buying one, there is a type that can only be operated with the cover in place. This seems safer to me than one that can be switched on while still open.

▥ Trailing cables from kettles, toasters and other appliances are a particular hazard. Many bad accidents have occurred from babies pulling kettles full of scalding hot liquid down on top of themselves. Until the manufacturers put safety before expediency, try to keep the cables short (it is a simple task for you or a handyman to shorten a cable, or take the appliance to your local electrical shop), tuck them to the back of the worktop or, better still, change to the new coiled cables.

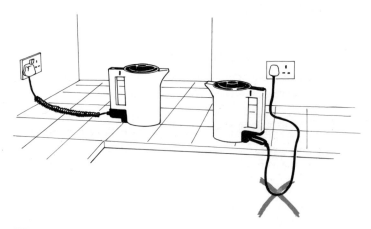

▥ Switch off any appliance at the socket before unplugging it (see *Electricity*, page 15).

Floors and surfaces

▥ Hard stone or tiled floors can get slippery when wet and cause falls. It might be worth temporarily covering such floors with cheap non-slip matting of some kind.

▥ Be aware of sharp edges and corners of kitchen cupboards when crawling and toddling start. Bubble-pack or corrugated cardboard taped over can be good padding, or you can buy special corner-protectors from babycare shops.

▓ Keep litter trays and pet food well away from crawling toddlers.

▓ Take great care when using a baby-walker, bouncing cradle or high chair in the kitchen. These cause many accidents (see *Falls*, page 18).

SITTING ROOM

This is statistically the most dangerous room in the house, falls and burns being the commonest accidents. It is a room where you will all spend a lot of time, and where hopefully you will be able to relax. It's worth trying to make it as safe as possible, so do read pages 7 to 49 which give lots of basic advice about preventing accidents. The following hazards are specific to sitting rooms, so they are covered here in more detail.

▓ Alcohol must be kept out of reach and out of sight or locked away. Toddlers tend to copy adults whom they have seen pouring out drinks. Don't leave your drink within reach of children – it can be 'down the hatch' in the blink of an eye.

▓ Don't leave cigarettes or cigarette ends lying around where they might be eaten by a curious toddler. Nicotine can cause nausea and diarrhoea if eaten (see page 41).

▓ Don't let children put newspapers or magazines in their mouths; although sucking newsprint is unlikely to poison, it may be the cause of an upset tummy.

▓ Fire-guards are essential with all types of fire (see *Fire*, page 25). If a child is burnt while alone in a room with an unguarded fire, you are liable to prosecution.

▥ Cover any sharp corners of low tables or chairs with temporary padding (see *Kitchen*, page 72).

▥ If you prop the baby up on the sofa with cushions, don't leave him alone: it's very easy for him to topple over and fall, or even to turn and suffocate.

▥ Try not to let the baby go near the back of the television set or touch any part of it; better to make it out of bounds from the start.

▓ This room will possibly have many sockets and trailing wires, particularly over Christmas, so follow the advice on page 15. Christmas tree lights must conform to BS 4647.

Houseplants

▓ Although there are no reported deaths from houseplant poisoning don't let the toddler eat the leaves or flowers of houseplants or cut flowers. Most are non-toxic but some can cause unpleasant upsets (see page 43).

▓ At Christmas time keep holly and mistletoe berries out of reach: both are poisonous and can cause tummy upsets if more than two or three are eaten.

STAIRS AND HALLWAYS

Stairs can be dangerous to a wobbly toddler, crawling baby or even younger child in a baby-walker. Unless you are confident he'll never reach them on his own, it's worth using safety gates or barriers at the top and bottom.

▓ Gates and barriers are made of wood or metal. Gates are permanent fixtures and need to be screwed to the wall, but they have the advantage of opening easily to let older children and adults get through. Barriers are simple to fix and rely on rubber buffer tension. Whichever type you get, measure up carefully so that you buy the right size. Make sure the gap between the floor and the lower edge of the gate or barrier is no more than 50 mm / 2 in or a baby could get his head stuck underneath. The bars must be no more than 85 mm / $3\frac{1}{2}$ in apart. Make regular checks to see the gate or barrier holds firm. Any barrier should conform to BS 4125.

▦ As soon as he starts crawling, begin teaching him to come downstairs backwards on his tummy. Our house is full of stairs and all my children learnt pretty quickly. If you have anywhere in the house with just one or two steps, that would be a good place to start. If you live in a flat or bungalow, it's worth practising 'stair lessons' in a friend's or relative's house.

▦ Don't let a toddler carry a glass or anything sharp up and down stairs, or carry large objects that may block his view and cause him to fall.

▦ Don't let babies use a baby-walker anywhere near stairs or steps – they can move very fast in them.

▦ Check that the stair carpet fits well and has no loose nails or rods. It's easy to slip while carrying the baby.

▨ If you have a modern house with stairs that have open treads with no risers, you will have to use stair carpet (even though it might look peculiar) until your child has grown too big to squeeze through the gaps.

▨ If some of your floors are rough or splintery, dress your baby in tough trousers when he reaches the crawling stage, and be ready to sew on knee patches!

▨ Take a good look at the banisters: are they close enough together to prevent squeezing through? Are there any loose or missing banisters?

▨ Look out for the very dangerous horizontal banisters that have been installed in many homes over the last few years; they are frequently too widely spaced and far too easy to climb up. You may need to board them over if they are really dangerous.

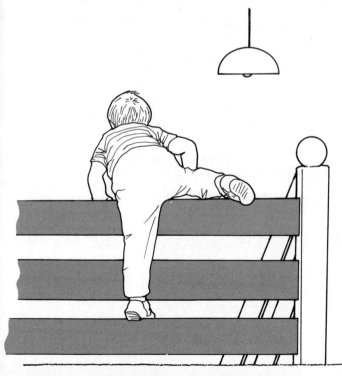

▦ Check for missing or broken handrails.

▦ A tiled floor at the bottom of the stairs can be dangerous: a friend of mine tripped and fell while carrying her baby downstairs and the baby's head was badly injured on the hard tiles at the bottom. Try to have underlay and carpet at the bottom, or at least a thick, *non-slip* rug.

▦ Front doors, if left open, are a danger – a crawling baby or one in a baby-walker can be out of the house and in the road very quickly if your back is turned.

WINDOWS, GLASS DOORS AND BALCONIES

There are many serious accidents caused by toddlers falling out of windows. And that's not the only danger: windows or glass doors can also be crashed through, causing terrible cuts. Don't assume that modern houses are designed to prevent these sorts of danger; architects in this country unfortunately still don't seem to put children's safety high on their list of priorities.

Windows

▦ Check all of them for broken sash-cords, faulty catches or broken or missing glass.

▦ Make sure none of the windows in the house can open too wide. If a sash window opens easily at the bottom, for instance, keep it locked. Ideally open sash windows only at the top when children are around.

▦ Fit safety catches to upstairs windows. These screw to the frame and prevent the window opening too wide. There are several types available. The maximum safe opening is about 100 mm/4 in.

▓ Watch out especially for the highly dangerous windows that pivot horizontally in the middle for cleaning. They can swing open if leant on. Many of these were installed in high-rise buildings and have caused fatal falls. If you have anything similar in your house or flat, check that there are safety catches and that they are in good working order. The catches must never be painted over.

▓ Don't put anything that a child can climb on near a window.

Glass doors or large low windows

▦ Toddlers can trip and fall or run through glass doors or windows and cut themselves very badly. Consider installing safety glass in all high-risk areas. Your local glass merchant will almost certainly suggest the laminated type (BS 6206) which is unfortunately very expensive. You may have to fit hardboard or polyester plastic safety film (BS 6206C) over the existing glass instead. This would be much cheaper, but make sure it is properly fitted and check it regularly.

▦ At the very least mark all large areas of glass with bright stickers, but don't rely on this to make it safe – children don't

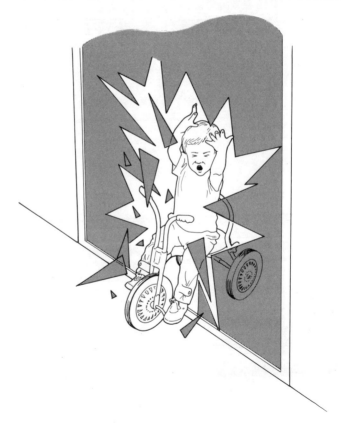

always look where they're going. In any case they can easily stumble and fall through even when they know the glass is there.

Balconies

There are many falls from dangerous balconies and if you have one it's essential that you check it for safety.

▨ Look carefully for any gaps that a toddler could squeeze through. If the bars are horizontal or spaced more than a few inches apart vertically, cover with fine wire netting, hardboard or perspex.

▨ Is the safety rail or wall high enough? It must be at least 900 mm / 3 ft. If not, extend it with hardboard or perspex.

▨ Is there a way of climbing over it? Never put anything on to the balcony which could be used as a ladder, like tubs or window boxes.

▨ If the balcony is not 100 per cent safe, keep the entrance on to it securely locked.

FIRST-AID BOX

It is sensible to keep a selection of basic first-aid equipment in the house. Keep it in a clean, dry, airtight box. Label it so it is quickly identifiable and keep it in a dry place – not the bathroom where it could be affected by steam.

1. Selection of differently sized sterile dressings. These now come attached to bandages, all ready to apply.
2. An assortment of sticking plasters.

3. A few rolls of cotton wool.
4. A packet of antiseptic wipes.
5. A selection of safety pins.
6. Tweezers.
7. A pair of blunt-ended scissors.
8. Thermometer.
9. Sachets of rehydrating powder, like Rehidrat or Dioralyte.

You may want to keep some children's paracetamol syrup somewhere ready to hand, but do make sure it is safely locked away.

If there is any condition your baby has which may need emergency treatment (allergies to bee stings or certain foods for instance), your doctor may recommend that you keep some quick first aid – such as antihistamine syrup – to hand. Check with the doctor if there is anything particular to your family that you should always have in the house.

SAFETY OUTSIDE THE HOME

THE CAR

It is only because people are still unaware of just how dangerous and damaging a car crash can be that so many babies and children travel unrestrained. Of course it's so easy to think 'just this once' and pop into the car holding your baby for a short journey, but please remember most accidents happen within a few miles of home. It's never worth risking it, however unlikely it seems that you will crash – how can you predict how other people on the road will drive?

By law everyone travelling in the front seat must wear a seat belt (ECE regulation 16). At the time of writing it looks certain that it will shortly also be against the law to carry young children unrestrained in the back of a car in which restraints are fitted. A baby must not be carried unrestrained on your lap, *even if you are belted*. Never be tempted into thinking a baby is safe in your arms or a sling – he is not, either in the front or back seat. The forces in a crash are so great that you simply could not hold on to the baby, and a sling would break, allowing the baby to be thrown through the windscreen or out of the car. The baby could even be crushed between you and the dashboard.

We must erase for ever the image of the maternity nurse placing baby in mother's arms in the car. From the moment you leave hospital . . . *strap him in*.

▥ Never carry your baby unrestrained in the car. There are loan schemes available for those who cannot afford to buy new equipment. About thirty such projects exist around the country; badger your health visitor to initiate such a scheme if there isn't one locally. There is a leaflet available from the Child Accident Prevention Trust (see page 170) on how to set up a loan scheme.

▥ Under no circumstances should you put a seat belt around yourself *and* the baby. The belt will not work properly and the baby could receive serious internal injuries.

▥ Be boring with friends and grandparents by insisting your baby is not allowed to travel without proper restraint and stick to it for the rest of his childhood (not easy once he gets invitations out to tea or joins a 'school run').

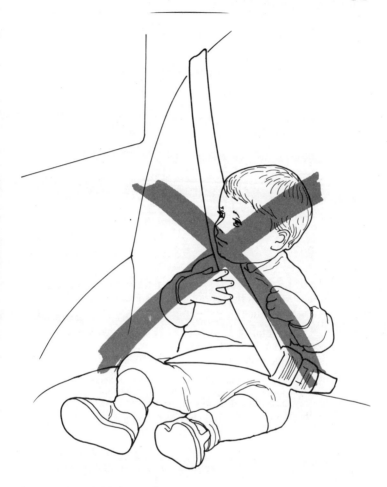

For a young baby, only one piece of equipment is now recommended by safety experts:

▦ Rear-facing infant carrier: these have only recently been introduced to Britain, having been successfully used abroad for many years. They are very safe and require no special fixing, being kept in place by an adult seat belt. Choose one that conforms to BS AU 202.

If you have rear seat belts, it is safest to put the carrier in the back. However, the front has the advantage of you and the baby being able to see each other without your having to keep looking behind you. I was once stopped by a police car and asked why I kept looking round: when he saw I had a screaming baby in the back he was very understanding, but it would have been much safer if I hadn't had to keep turning round.

▥ You may have heard of the carry-cot restraint. This is a specially fitted harness that straps around a carry-cot on the back seat. If you have one, make sure it conforms to BS AU 186. Nowadays, however, it is no longer considered really safe. The safety depends solely on the strength of the carry-cot itself and the baby can easily be thrown out in a crash. If you do use one, make certain the carry-cot cover is in place.

To sum up, the order of safety is:

● Rear-facing infant carrier in the back

● Rear-facing infant carrier in the front

● Restrained carry-cot in the back (not satisfactory, but better than nothing).

Remember: unrestrained in the back is not safe, and unrestrained in the front is extremely unsafe and illegal.

▓ As the baby gets older (eight to nine months, or around 9 to 10 kg / 20 to 24 lb and can sit up unaided), you will have to change to a child safety seat. Make sure it conforms to BS 3254 or EEC regulation 44, that it is properly fitted and that you always use it. There will almost certainly come a time when your child will rebel and you may have to go through some full-scale tantrums. (I did – at times it was like trying to push a very strong, yelling conger eel into a small cardboard box. If he'd been old enough to know any obscenities, I hate to think what he would have been calling me.) Don't ever be tempted to give in. Remember, his life may be at stake; once he accepts the inevitability of the seat's use, you will have no more trouble.

Make sure the seat is easily cleaned; you're bound to have a few accidents once he's out of nappies, and the amount of rusk crumbs, milk spills and squashed orange segments that can creep down the sides is unbelievable.

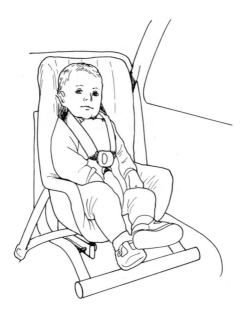

▦ Tempting as it may be as a good way of keeping him quiet, it's not really safe to feed the baby while the car is moving – he might choke. Only give him food or drink when you're sitting with him while the car is stationary.

▦ Child locks, which are fitted on some cars, are not really necessary for children under the age of three as they will be restrained in child safety seats and so unable to reach the doors. When the children are older, they might possibly be able to reach the handles if they are wearing inertia-reel seat belts so the locks might be useful. However, by this time they should be well-trained and know better than to fiddle with the doors while the car is moving.

▦ A child's seat belt (BS 3254) is relatively inexpensive and easy to fit. You can buy one from car-accessory shops or large babycare stores.

▦ Children over the age of three can be restrained with an ordinary adult seat belt as long as you use a specially manufactured booster cushion.

▦ Always wear a seat belt yourself, even in the back seat. If there are no belts fitted in the back consider having them installed if you can afford it. (I wish all car safety equipment were provided free by the government.) Do remember, however well your baby is strapped in, he is still in danger if there is an unrestrained adult in the same car. Anyone not wearing a seat belt can become a deadly missile in a crash. In a horrific accident recently, a mother who was unstrapped not only died herself but also killed her husband and her baby with the weight of her flying body. Everyone must be strapped in. Even dogs should ideally be restrained for the same reason, but this is hardly practical, so guard rails are a good idea in estate cars or hatchbacks. In saloons, sit the dog on the floor behind the front seats.

▦ Keep a first-aid kit in your car. Apart from a thermometer, it should contain the same items as your home first-aid kit.

▦ Keep your car well maintained, regularly serviced and in a safe condition.

Other dangers

▦ Be very careful not to shut your baby's fingers in the car door: try to get in the habit of always checking to see where his hand is before you slam the door.

▦ It is dangerous to leave your baby alone in the car, even for a short time. Apart from the nightmare possibility of someone taking the baby, there have been tragic incidents of babies overheating when left in sunny supermarket car parks while Mum was shopping in the air-conditioned inside. Occasionally electrical faults have caused cars to burst into flame. Recently one did so with a young child inside and she could not be rescued because the car was locked.

▦ You can buy roller blinds which fix to the back windows of the car to protect baby from overheating on long summer journeys. Alternatively, a towelling nappy or any piece of material tucked into the top of a side window is an effective 'sunshade', or there are dark perspex panels that fit to the window by suction to give shade where you need it.

(See also *Travel*, page 104.)

THE STREET

▦ Choose your pram carefully, making sure it conforms to BS 4139. If you are getting a secondhand one, check that it is sturdy, the brakes work on a slope and it has a place to attach a safety harness.

▦ As soon as the baby can sit up, a harness should always be used. Falls out of prams are very common. Buy one that conforms to BS 6684.

▦ In cold weather a baby can lose heat quickly, even in a pram and particularly from his head. Keep him well wrapped and his head covered in cold weather and protect him from draughts, using the pram hood if it is windy. Feel his skin under the covers to see if he is warm enough. Although fresh air is good for a healthy baby, it's probably not so important when he has a cold or the weather is foggy or very cold.

▦ In hot weather it is important that the baby doesn't get too hot; he should be kept out of direct sunlight, with the pram hood down and a sun canopy. Again, feel his skin under his clothes to check if he is comfortable. If he is very hot and sweaty, remove some covering or take him inside somewhere cool.

▦ If using a pushchair or buggy, check that it conforms to BS 4792: it will then have two separate locking devices so one can act as a failsafe.

▦ Make sure your buggy is well maintained, and do try not to carry heavy shopping slung over the back. I know we all do it, but it does weaken the structure, and if it becomes faulty, little fingers may get trapped. Also it can overbalance if the shopping is very heavy. There are pushchairs made now with shopping baskets underneath. Don't expect a buggy necessarily to be usable for a second baby. It would need a thorough overhaul and might not be safe enough.

▦ When you're out with the baby in the pushchair, be aware of idiots who throw burning cigarette ends out of their car windows; one landed in the lap of a friend's baby the other day. If the mother hadn't noticed, the baby could have been badly burnt.

▥ Always do up the safety strap and preferably use a harness as well.

Road accidents (pedestrian)

▥ Crossing the road with a baby in a pram or buggy can be a tricky manoeuvre. Don't 'test the water' by pushing it out into the road ahead of you before you can really see if it's clear. Always choose a safe place to cross where you can clearly see if there's anything coming. If you must cross near parked vehicles, peer around them yourself first and only push out the pram or buggy when all is clear.

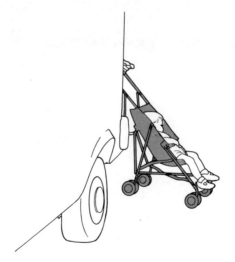

▥ If you're unloading from a car, always take out any shopping, coats and toys before you take out your child; once he is walking it's only too easy to put him on the pavement then dive back in the car to fetch your things while he is tottering into the road. This very nearly happened to me once and I still shudder when I think how close I came to disaster.

▥ Always get your child out on the pavement side of the car.

▥ A toddler tends to dart into the road when out walking. Reins (BS 3785 or BS 6684) can be extremely helpful here. (Some parents complain that putting a child in reins is unkind and unnecessarily restrictive. If you feel this way, be sure you always keep a constant firm hold on your child's hand.)

▥ Start teaching your child good road sense as soon as possible, always stopping at the kerb and telling him to look both ways, then carrying him across or holding his hand firmly, however small the road you are crossing. When the rebellious stage is reached, stay firm, if necessary dragging him screaming and kicking across the road but never letting go of his hand.

▦ Set your child a good example by always choosing the safest place to cross, such as zebra crossings and subways. The ability to judge the speed and location of traffic is a skill that takes a long time to develop, and a child is not totally reliable as a pedestrian in traffic until the age of about twelve.

THE PLAYGROUND

Places of fun are often full of dangers, particularly for very young children. Toddlers can easily walk in front of swings, for example, or misjudge the speed of a roundabout.

▦ Teach toddlers to keep well away from rides, unless you or another adult is with them.

▦ Try to use playgrounds that have soft surfaces under the equipment and swing seats made of plastic, rubber or wood.

▦ Watch all the time – it's easy to get chatting to a friend and let your child walk into danger.

▦ Little fingers can easily catch in bicycle wheels. Look out for older children's bikes that may be propped up in the playground and played with by an inquisitive toddler.

▦ Hold on to the baby at the top of a slide, and don't let him climb up one that is too high for you to reach. Always make sure there is at least an arm's length between children sliding down. Some children find it easier to come down feet first on their tummies.

▦ When he is on the swing, teach him to sit well in the middle and to hold on with both hands, never to kneel or stand.

▦ If the equipment in your local playground isn't safe, report it at once to your local council.

THE GARDEN, PARK OR COUNTRYSIDE

Garden

▦ Garden gates must be kept securely closed so that the baby cannot get out on to the road. If necessary fit a lock that the baby cannot open.

▦ Garden sheds and garages may contain dangerous chemicals, sharp blades and tools, so keep them locked and out of bounds.

▦ Be aware of dangerous equipment such as electrical hedge trimmers, lawnmowers or ladders left lying in the garden.

▦ Don't leave anything sharp or poisonous lying around.

▦ Check that any outdoor play equipment is safe, and that swings and climbing frames are on soft surfaces.

▦ Be aware of the terrible dangers of unfenced water (see *Drowning*, page 13).

▦ Whether you have a cat of your own or not, always use a cat net when the baby is out in the garden in the pram.

▦ If you have a dog, make sure it is regularly wormed and that bowel movements are done in as hygienic a way as possible. Dog faeces can contain the parasite *Toxacara canis* which, if picked up on the fingers and eaten, can cause blindness in children. Although this outcome is extremely rare, teach your toddler never to touch faeces. There are special units available for the safe disposal of dog mess. They are a bit like chemical lavatories: you dig them into your garden and shovel the mess into them as necessary.

Poisonous plants

Many children are admitted to hospital with suspected poisoning after having eaten parts of plants but in the experience of the National Poison Information Service almost all of them suffer no symptoms at all, or at worst mild tummy upsets. Plant poisoning is a subject that worries many parents quite disproportionately. It's ironic that many people will take enormous trouble to prevent laburnum poisoning, which has caused not a single child death this century, while they will quite happily drive around with their children unstrapped in the car (the cause of about 500 deaths every year).

▓ Most plants are non-toxic but it's still a good idea to teach your toddler never to eat anything out of the garden.

▓ Try not to grow berry-bearing plants (although the ones people often worry about – *Cotoneaster* and *Pyracantha* – are very low in toxicity).

▓ If there is a tree or plant in your garden that worries you (such as yew perhaps), it's worth fencing it in until the child is old enough to be trusted not to eat any of it. Colourful berries and flowers can be very tempting to small children, and illustrated below are some of the garden plants that can be harmful if eaten, but do remember serious reactions are very rare. In all suspected cases of poisoning from plants, take a sample of the plant with you to the hospital to aid identification and help in the choice of treatment.

The illustrations overleaf show some of the more common garden plants that may cause a reaction.

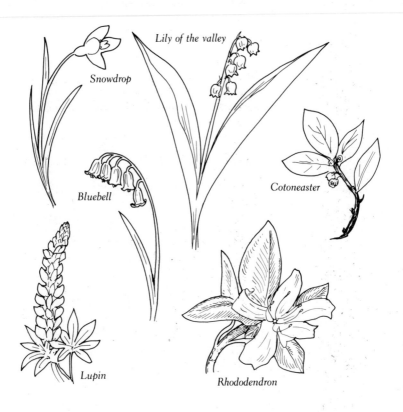

Snowdrop

Lily of the valley

Bluebell

Cotoneaster

Lupin

Rhododendron

Bluebell (*Endymion* spp.), January–September. The root bulbs and fruits are poisonous; 6 to 10 pods can cause diarrhoea.

Cotoneaster (*Cotoneaster* spp.). A bush bearing red berries popularly believed to be poisonous. This is not so; the berries are low in toxicity.

Holly (*Ilex aquifolium*), October–January. The red berries can be deadly if eaten by children.

Larkspur/Delphinium (*Delphinium* spp.), April–September. May have blue, white or mauvish-red flowers. All species are poisonous, particularly young plants and seeds, but no deaths have been reported.

Lily of the valley (*Convallaria majalis*), April–August. All parts of the plant are toxic, and even the water from a vase containing these flowers can poison.

Privet

Larkspur

Holly

Pyracantha

Morning glory

Wisteria

Lupin (*Lupinus* spp.), May–October. Children often mistake the furry seed pods of this flower for pea-pods. Symptoms are similar to laburnum, but not so severe.

Morning glory (*Ipomoea purpurea*), July–October. Seeds contain hallucinogenic LSD and can cause permanent brain damage if eaten.

Privet (*Ligustrum* spp.), August–October. Berries and leaves are poisonous; highly dangerous if eaten in large amounts.

Pyracantha/Firethorn (*Pyracantha* spp.). The red berries of this bush are low in toxicity, despite a common belief to the contrary.

Rhododendron (*Rhododendron* spp.), May–July. All parts can cause poisoning.

Wisteria (*Wisteria* spp.), July–November. 1 or 2 seeds may cause a toxic reaction in children. Symptoms usually pass in 24 hours.

Snowdrop (*Galanthus nivalis*), April–October. The whole plant contains toxic substances, but spontaneous recovery usually occurs in a few hours.

Parks and countryside

▦ Don't let your toddler wander off alone to explore in the park or countryside.

▦ Don't encourage your toddler to stroke every dog he meets, unless you are assured of its temperament by the owner. Encourage a healthy respect for the unknown responses of all animals, but without instilling unnecessary fear. Remember dogs tend to be irritable if carrying a bone or anything in their mouths.

▦ Remember the danger from dog faeces (see *Garden*, page 94). Take a rug or cloth with you to sit on. Don't let baby put anything in his mouth and wash his hands thoroughly when you get home if he has been crawling on the grass or playing in the sandpit.

▦ Snake bites are very rare, but there are occasionally cases of toddlers being bitten. Once they are walking, make sure they wear boots in heathland areas where there may be adders (the *only* poisonous snakes in Great Britain, see page 161).

▦ When there is clover in flower on the grass, don't let the baby run around in bare feet – there may well be bees.

▦ Teach him to stand still and keep calm if a bee is buzzing round him; panic only makes it worse. Keep his face clean of sweet stickiness, especially round the mouth, and don't allow him to walk around with a tempting jam sandwich if there are bees or wasps about.

▦ Swans and geese can attack if provoked so don't let your toddler too near them when feeding the ducks. My youngest was even scratched by a peacock in a London park last year. I'm not sure which of them was more surprised . . .

Wild plants

There are a few basic rules about plants in the countryside which should keep you and your child safe.

Our illustrations show some of the wild poisonous plants more commonly eaten by children, but do remember that in the vast majority of cases there is no reaction, or at worst a slight tummy upset. If in any doubt, always telephone your doctor. In all suspected cases of poisoning from plants, take a sample of the plant with you to the hospital to aid identification and help in the choice of treatment.

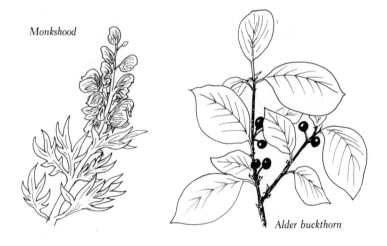

Monkshood

Alder buckthorn

Aconite/Monkshood (*Aconitum napellus*). Perennial with bluish-mauve flowers. Poisonous seeds, but no reported fatalities.
Alder buckthorn/Black alder (*Frangula alnus*), April–September. Poisonous purplish-black berries. Twigs are also toxic if chewed. Symptoms are usually mild.
Black bryony (*Tamus communis*), July–October. This plant's shiny green berries, which become red when ripe, can cause blistering of the mouth followed by vomiting and diarrhoea.

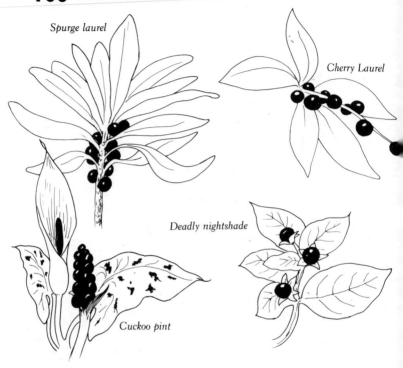

Spurge laurel

Cherry Laurel

Deadly nightshade

Cuckoo pint

Black or garden nightshade (*Solanum nigrum*), May–October. All parts of the plant are poisonous, particularly unripe berries; ripe berries, which can be green, red or black, are usually less toxic and a few can be eaten with no apparent ill-effects.

Cherry laurel (Prunus laurocerasus). A shrub with shiny oblong pointed leaves and small berries which turn black when ripe. See **Spurge laurel**.

Cuckoo pint/Lords and ladies (*Arum maculatum*), April–September. The reddish-orange berries, which ripen in autumn, are very poisonous. The leaves can also cause a toxic reaction.

Deadly nightshade (*Atropa belladonna*), May–October. Relatively uncommon now; more than 5 of the black berries can cause severe, sometimes fatal, poisoning.

Death cap (*Amanita phalloides*), June–October. Highly poisonous. Symptoms develop 6 to 24 hours after eating.

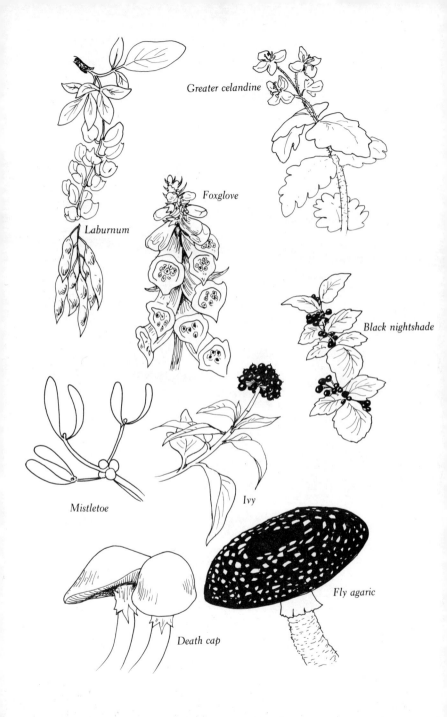

Greater celandine

Laburnum

Foxglove

Black nightshade

Mistletoe

Ivy

Death cap

Fly agaric

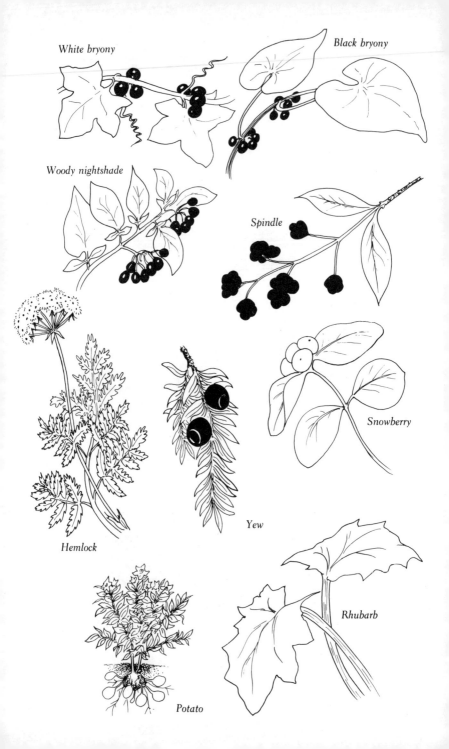

White bryony

Black bryony

Woody nightshade

Spindle

Snowberry

Yew

Hemlock

Potato

Rhubarb

Fly agaric (*Amanita muscaria*), late February–early July and September–November. Distinctive red and white cap. Dangerous but not usually deadly. Symptoms develop within 1½ hours of eating.

Foxglove (*Digitalis purpurea*), March–September. The purple flowers are toxic if eaten; children have also been poisoned by drinking the water from vases containing these flowers.

Greater celandine (*Chelidonium majus*), April–September. The pods contain white-tipped black seeds and are highly toxic. The sap can cause skin irritation.

Hemlock (*Conium maculatum*), April–August. The whole plant is poisonous and can cause death.

Ivy (*Hedera helix*). Perennial with poisonous leaves and berries.

Laburnum (*Laburnum anagyroides*), April–November. All parts of the tree, particulary the bark and seeds, are poisonous; 15 seeds can be fatal. Symptoms develop in less than 1 hour.

Mistletoe (*Viscum album*), September–February. 3 to 4 berries may cause mild toxic symptoms.

Potato (*Solanum tuberosum*), May–October. Stems, stalks and fruit can cause poisoning if eaten.

Rhubarb (*Rheum* spp.), April–September. The raw leaves and stalks are toxic; even when cooked, the leaves can cause severe, sometimes fatal, poisoning.

Snowberry (*Symphoricarpos rivularis*), August–December. More than 2 berries can cause vomiting, dizziness and mild sedation in children.

Spindle (*Euonymus europaeus*), April–October. The dark pink fruit capsules which split open when ripe, revealing a bright orange fleshy substance, are poisonous. Symptoms appear 10 to 12 hours after eating and can be very severe if large amounts have been eaten.

Spurge laurel (*Daphne laureola*). This perennial bush has oval green berries which become black when fully ripe. Children sometimes mistake them for currants. Their bitter taste usually prevents many being eaten, so symptoms are generally mild.

White bryony (*Bryonia dioica*), May–August. The dull red berries contain black and yellow mottled seeds which are mildly toxic.

Woody nightshade (*Solanum dulcamara*), April–October. This plant has oval green berries which become red when ripe. Over 6 berries can cause drowsiness and paralysis; more can cause death.

Yew (*Taxus baccata*), July–October. The red fleshy fruit is of low toxicity, but the leaves and black seeds, if chewed well, are very poisonous.

▥ Don't let him pick blackberries and eat them until he is at least five years old, in case he gets confused about what is safe.

▥ Don't pick wild mushrooms unless you're *absolutely* sure of what you're doing: many poisonous toadstools look very similar to the edible ones.

▥ Reactions to poisons of all kinds vary widely so it's not possible to give exact advice about how much of a certain substance will cause symptoms. The notorious, but luckily very rare, Deadly Nightshade can kill if enough berries are eaten, but a housewife who recently baked and ate a 'bilberry' pie lived to tell the tale . . .

Fireworks

▥ Never let babies or young children anywhere near fireworks before, during or after they are set off.

▥ Make sure fireworks are stored somewhere safe, or even better don't buy any at all and take the family to a properly organized public display.

OTHER PEOPLE'S HOUSES

You can't rely on someone else's sense of safety, particularly if the person doesn't have a young child. The only way to be sure is to watch your baby all the time and be aware of any possible hazards. Remember other people may leave their hot tea near the edge of a low table, keep scissors in an easily opened drawer and so on: never relax!

If you leave your baby at a friend's house, try to leave an address or telephone number where you can be contacted (see also page 32).

TRAVEL

▓ Don't forget to pack a sunscreen and any medication the baby may need while away. Also make sure you take sterilizing tablets or solution if you are using them.

▓ Some areas are unsuitable for young babies. When I asked Dr G. C. Cook from the Hospital for Tropical Diseases, London, what advice he would give to families with young babies travelling to malarious areas, he said emphatically that it would be 'Don't!' Apparently, more and more areas are infected with drug-resistant parasites, and the anti-malarial drugs can have serious side-effects, especially in young babies. If it is important that you travel to such an area, ask your doctor's advice.

▓ Most baby milks are available all over the world but may be more expensive. It is possible that in some tropical areas the baby milks sold could be very different from those in Europe. If in doubt, take some with you.

▓ Dried baby foods can be very useful on holiday. If your baby has not had them before, start getting him used to them before you go.

▓ Take a first-aid kit whenever you travel abroad. This should be the same basic kit you keep at home (see page 81), but you should add calamine for sunburn or insect bites. Sachets of Rehidrat or Dioralyte are essential as holiday diarrhoea is all too common and can lead to dehydration.

▓ If the baby will need several bottle feeds on a journey, take them cold in a thermos and pour them out as necessary, or take boiled water and mix them up as needed. Never keep milk warm – this is highly dangerous as bacteria can breed very quickly.

▓ If travelling by car, please make sure everyone is properly restrained (see pages 83–88).

▓ If your toddler is always travel-sick, try giving him something light to eat an hour or so before you leave. Alternatively, ask your doctor if he would recommend Dramamine; the manufacturers say it can be taken by children aged as young as one year. (My niece has been much helped by the bands, available from chemists, that exert pressure on a point on the inside of the wrist. Whether it's just because she believes they work I don't know but they do appear to be effective.) Travel-sickness is unpleasant (for everybody in the car) but is not dangerous and the child will almost certainly grow out of it.

There is no reason why a baby should not be taken abroad at a very young age, although flying is not safe during the first two days of life – the heart and lungs are not ready to cope with the reduced oxygen concentration. Some doctors feel it is a wise precaution not to go until the triple immunization (diphtheria, tetanus and polio, see page 31) has been started, but check with your own doctor.

Before you go abroad you should almost certainly take out some medical insurance. Most European countries and some others provide free medical care to UK citizens (see DHSS leaflet SA 30 'Medical Costs Abroad') but the care provided may be limited and complicated to apply for. Holiday health insurance is normally very reasonably priced and well worth having: ask your travel agent.

Check with your doctor for any immunizations your baby might need. There is a booklet available (DHSS SA 35 'Protect Your Health Abroad') giving details of what is required, but you must always check with your doctor as a new epidemic of an infectious disease can occur at any time. Make sure you find out inoculation requirements at least six weeks before your holiday – many people leave immuniza-tions to the last minute. The immunizations for typhoid, cholera and yellow fever are not recommended for babies under one year old so, if possible, it's worth avoiding travel to countries that require them until the baby is older.

If your baby has a heavy cold or an ear infection, it is not a good idea to fly – the change in pressure in the aeroplane could cause intense pain in his ears. Do ask your doctor's advice.

▓ Even if your baby has no cold, he may experience discomfort in his ears during ascent and descent owing to the change in pressure. Let him suck on a dummy or have a feed – the sucking and swallowing will help his ears.

▓ Let the airline know in advance that you will be travelling with a young baby and ask for the bulkhead seats which have room for a carry-cot. Airlines often insist that you use theirs, but they must be requested when reserving your tickets.

▓ After landing do follow the instructions of the air hostess not to stand up until the plane has come to a complete stop. Most people ignore this completely, and many are injured as a consequence. Sit safely with your baby until told to undo your seat belt. (Families with young children are frequently given priority in boarding and leaving aeroplanes; ask the stewardess.)

On holiday – outside

▓ Keep your child in the shade when possible. Young skin burns very easily indeed so use plenty of high-protection sun cream. For fair-skinned families like mine the new creams have revolutionized holidays. My childhood was spent covered in calamine or swimming in long-sleeved shirts.

▓ Avoid the midday sun. Apart from the pain of sunburn we now know that over-exposure to the sun in childhood can sometimes cause skin cancer in later life.

▓ Keep the baby in loose cotton clothes; remember he can get burnt even when the sky is overcast. Every year far too many children are taken to hospital with severe burns from the sun.

▓ If your baby is in a pram or buggy, keep the hood down and use a canopy: don't let him get overheated. If he's more than a few months old, judge the amount of clothing he should wear by what you feel comfortable in.

▦ Make sure the baby has plenty of water to drink in hot weather, particularly if he is sweating. If he won't drink, let him suck a sponge (specially bought) soaked in clean water.

▦ If the sun is very bright you may need to shade baby's eyes. Sunglasses are unsatisfactory for babies or toddlers as they seldom fit well and fall off easily; it's much better to have a hat with a brim to shield his eyes. This is more likely to stay on and will also protect his head and the skin of his face.

When our daughter was tiny, I pushed her pram along a bumpy beach in France and the hood bounced down; the sun went straight in her eyes and she screamed terrifyingly as if in pain. We rushed her to the nearest doctor (very French, very handsome and very expensive) who reassured us that all was well, but I've been careful about sun ever since (and about checking holiday medical insurance).

▦ If a toddler refuses to wear a hat, don't worry too much about his eyes, but wet his head every now and then to keep it cool.

▦ Hold his hand while he's paddling. Don't fall asleep and let him wander down to the water on his own. Some parents take an inflatable paddling pool so their toddler can splash around in relative safety – never take your eyes off a child playing in or near water.

▦ Look out for unexpected hazards – broken glass, poisonous plants (see pages 96–103) or deep holes. (Remember the frightening story of the little girl who fell down an unused well in America recently.)

▦ Watch for dogs and insects. If you are abroad you must keep your child away from all animals – there is a real risk of catching rabies from a bite or scratch.

▦ Don't let a wobbly toddler walk around with a lolly in his mouth. He could trip and force the stick down the back of his throat.

In the hotel, guest house or restaurant

▦ Check your room for all dangers as outlined in *Safety in the Home* (see pages 50–82).

▦ Watch out, especially if you are abroad, for dangerous cots and heaters. Both are made to different standards from BSIs and you may find the cot bars too widely spaced and the fire inadequately guarded. Travel cots may be flimsy, so keep a close eye once your baby begins to be active.

▦ Don't use your own hairdryer, iron or other electrical equipment unless you are sure that it is safe to do so. Most UK appliances can be used on the Continent quite safely if you use an adaptor.

▦ Never leave tins of baby food half eaten, especially in hot weather. Throw them away. Packets of dried food are a more economical and safer alternative.

▦ Most northern European towns have tap water that is safe to drink and for mixing feeds, but in rural areas and other countries it may be contaminated. If in any doubt, play safe. Boil the tap water for ten minutes and then let it cool. Teeth must be brushed in boiled water, and only use ice made from safe water.

Don't use bottled water for babies, either for drinking or in the feeds; it is not sterile and may contain too many minerals.

If in a country where the standards of hygiene are suspect, only give toddlers wrapped ice-creams and fruit which has been peeled or washed in safe water.

Don't let children eat shellfish – it's not worth the risk.

Toddlers must only drink milk which is boiled, pasteurized or UHT.

Be extra careful about sterilizing and, if self-catering, wipe down worktops with sterilizing solution when preparing food.

Check your fire-escape route. Some hotels abroad may not have the same standard of arrangements for escape as do UK hotels.

Toys abroad may not conform to the equivalent of British safety standards, so take extra care (see also page 48).

As at home, it's worth assuming the worst may happen and finding the number of the local doctor, A and E department or paediatric service. Or just knowing there is someone you could turn to in an emergency. Mondial Assistance or Europ Assistance offer very good value (see page 174).

II.

EMERGENCY ACTION

EMERGENCY PRIORITIES

In any emergency your priorities are:

I. Safety

Remove the baby from danger or the danger from the baby, making sure you too are safe.

2. ABC

Learn the life-saving procedures of checking *Airway – Breathing – Circulation* (see page 116), what to do when the baby is *Choking* (see page 127) and how to stop *Bleeding* (see page 126).

3. Summon Medical Help

Telephone your family doctor or dial 999 for an ambulance or get someone to drive you and the baby to your nearest Accident and Emergency department. Try to avoid driving yourself in an emergency: you would be upset, it would be dangerous and there would be no one to look after the baby and watch his condition.

If the baby is seriously ill, it's nearly always best to dial 999 immediately. Ambulances are extremely well equipped nowadays and the ambulance attendants fully trained to carry out many life-saving and emergency procedures on the way to hospital, thus saving valuable time.

● In any emergency it is officially recommended you try to take a note of the time the incident happened, and if at all possible write down everything you do. Most of us would probably be far too upset and panicky to do so, but it's worth trying; it helps to keep you calm and could be valuable information for the doctors.

- Keep talking to your baby, reassure him and try to calm him. Most emergencies are happily resolved and a calm positive attitude will help your baby to feel less frightened.

- When you get to the hospital, keep talking to him. Calmly tell the doctor exactly what has happened. They will examine the baby in your arms or on your knee if at all possible, and many toddlers will feel more secure if their vests are left on during the examination.

- If your toddler hates having sticky plasters taken off as much as mine do, it may be worth asking if they could use surgical tape to secure any dressings.

- DO NOT TRY TO GIVE YOUR CHILD ANYTHING TO EAT OR DRINK IN AN EMERGENCY IN CASE HE NEEDS AN ANAESTHETIC LATER.

LIFE-SAVING PROCEDURES
ABC
(AIRWAY – BREATHING – CIRCULATION)
BLEEDING
CHOKING

Important: the brain needs oxygen. If a baby stops breathing, brain damage may occur in only a few minutes.

Heavy blood loss in a young baby is dangerous.

Every parent should know the following three life-saving procedures. Read and learn them thoroughly, but do not try any of them out on your baby. The only way to practise is on a proper model on a first-aid course (see page 130).

Some of the following may appear repetitive, but will save you cross-referring in a panic.

AIRWAY –
BREATHING –
CIRCULATION

If the baby appears to be unconscious and/or not breathing, this is what you must do. Start immediately – every second counts.

A – Airway

You must open his airway so he can breathe. This is vital and often alone prevents any breathing problem:

▒ Sit down. Put baby face up over your knee or on the table with his head over the edge.

▒ Support his head gently on your hand.

▒ Lift the bony part of his chin with the fingers of your other hand. This stops the tongue dropping back and blocking the airway. Don't press into the soft part under his chin as this will force the tongue into the airway.

▒ Clear his mouth carefully with your fingers of any obvious food, toy, vomit or other obstruction.

Now look, listen and feel to see if he is breathing.

▒ Put your ear to his mouth so you can hear and feel any breath

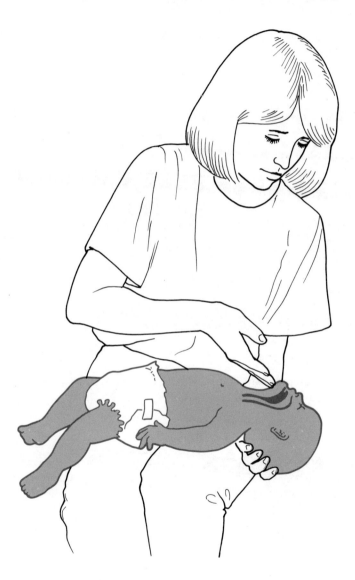

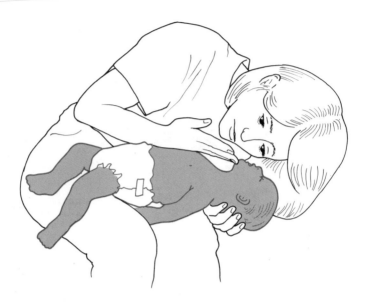

on your cheek, while looking to see if his chest is moving up and down.

▥ If he is breathing, turn him over as a unit and lie him on his tummy on the floor or bed, making sure his head is to the side and tilted back so his airway is open.

▐ Stay with him until help arrives. Any baby that has been unconscious *must* be seen by a doctor.

B – Breathing

If he is not breathing, you must breathe for him: you breathe out enough oxygen to keep him alive.

▐ Keeping his head tilted back to maintain an open airway, place your mouth to cover baby's nose and mouth (or if a toddler, pinch his nose shut and cover just his mouth with yours).

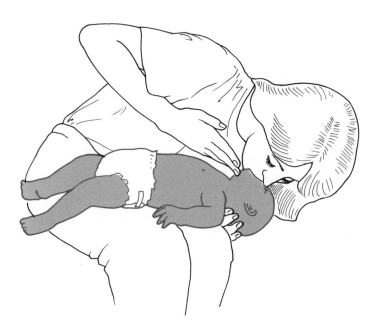

▨ Blow gently into his mouth and nose (or mouth alone), watching to see that his chest rises. *Stop as soon as you see it do so.* Don't over-inflate.

▨ Take your mouth off while you watch to see his chest fall as the air comes out again.

If his chest doesn't rise when you blow, see ☆ page 123.)

▨ Give him two breaths in this way, then check circulation.

C – Circulation

Check that his heart is beating:

▨ Try to find his pulse on the inside of his upper arm, between elbow and shoulder. With your thumb on the outside of his arm, press your index and middle fingers gently into the groove below the biceps muscle until a pulse is felt.

▦ If you feel a pulse, continue breathing for him until help arrives or he can breathe on his own. Do one breath for him like this about every three seconds.

▦ If you can't feel a pulse, or if it is very slow – less than one beat per second – you must start heart compression.

Heart compressions

▦ Feel for the bottom of his ribs and find the place where they join in the middle at the bottom of his breast bone. You are going to press down one finger's breadth above that place, on his breast bone.

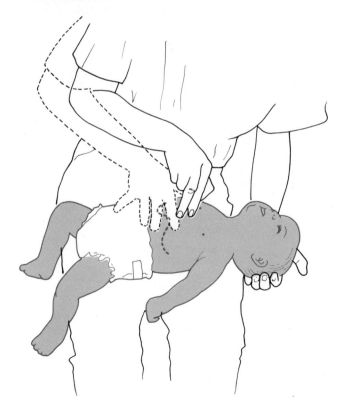

▦ Use two fingers over the correct place and press just hard enough to push down 1–2 cm/½–1 in (2–2½ cm/1–1½ in for a toddler). Do this smoothly and evenly, just faster than once a second (about a hundred times a minute).

▦ Let the chest return to its normal height between pushes but don't lift your fingers off. Don't jerk.

▦ Feel for his pulse with your other hand while you're pressing. If you can't feel it, then press harder.

▦ After every five presses, give him one breath, then another five presses and so on.

▦ If there is someone with you (and they have already called for help) get them to take over the heart compressions while you do the breathing. Tell them to count in fives as they do it, pausing after every fifth press to let you fill up baby's lungs.

▦ Keep checking the pulse.

▦ Carry on until the heart starts beating on its own or help arrives.

▦ Once the heart is beating, continue mouth-to-mouth breathing until he can breathe on his own or help arrives.

▦ Once he is breathing on his own but still unconscious or very sleepy, turn him as a unit on to his front or side on the floor or bed, his head to the side and tilted back to keep his airway open. This is very important: if you leave him lying on his back, his airway could easily be blocked by his tongue or by vomit.

▦ Continue to check his A–B–C. Never leave a baby alone when unconscious.

✼
If his chest didn't rise when you gave him mouth-to-mouth breathing:

▥ Check his airway again – are you sure his head is tilted back enough? Try repositioning the head. Can you see any obstruction?

▥ Try another breath. If still no good, there may be an obstruction lower down. Try to dislodge it as follows:

Back blows

Small baby:

▥ Lie him face down along your arm which is braced against your body, his head tilted downwards and supported by your hand firmly holding his jaw. Bang him sharply high between the shoulder blades four times with the heel of your hand.

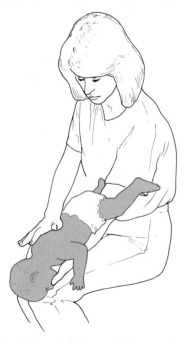

Toddler or large baby:

 Put him over your knee, tilted head down, and bang him high between the shoulder blades sharply about four times with the heel of your hand. This should dislodge the object. Try breathing for him again. You may have moved something without knowing it.

░░░░ If this doesn't work, place your free hand on baby's back so he is sandwiched between two hands. While continuing to support his head and neck, turn him over as a unit and place him on your thigh, his head lower than his trunk, and perform four chest thrusts.

Chest thrusts

░░░░ Feel for the bottom of his ribs and find where they join in the middle at the bottom of his breastbone. Measure one finger's breadth above this place so you are over the lower part of the breastbone.

░░░░ With two or three fingers, depending on his size, press down firmly but not jerkily to a depth of 1–2 cm/$\frac{1}{2}$–1 in, letting the chest come up again after each push, but not taking your fingers off. Do four of these chest thrusts slightly faster than one a second.

░░░░ Open baby's mouth by grasping both the tongue and lower jaw between the thumb and finger and lifting. Check in his mouth to see if there is anything easily removable, but don't just stick your finger blindly down his throat – that may make things worse.

░░░░ Turn him on to his back and try two more mouth-to-mouth breaths.

░░░░ Then do four more back blows.

░░░░ Then do four more chest thrusts.

░░░░ Repeat this procedure until his chest rises as you give him mouth-to-mouth; then keep breathing for him until he can breathe on his own.

░░░░ Check his circulation as above.

BLEEDING

If the baby is bleeding badly, it is important to try to stop it.

▓ Check airway and breathing first: remember your A–B–C.

▓ Shout for someone to dial 999 for an ambulance if you are not alone.

▓ Remove any obvious pieces of glass or foreign body, but if something is deeply embedded and oozing, *leave it alone* – it may be plugging the wound and preventing serious bleeding.

▓ Press hard with your fingers directly on the wound (use a clean dressing soaked in water if you have one, but don't waste time).

▓ Raise the wound above the level of the heart at the same time if possible. You will have to steel yourself and ignore his screams as it may hurt him, but it's important to press hard enough to stop the bleeding.

If the bleeding comes in spurts it is probably coming from an artery. Press between the bleeding point and the heart to slow it.

Keep pressing until the bleeding is controlled or help arrives. If the bleeding comes through the dressing don't remove it – add more layers.

Dial 999 for an ambulance now if you're on your own.

Keep baby warm and talk to him comfortingly until help arrives. He must go to hospital as soon as possible – babies do not tolerate blood loss well.

Don't give him anything to eat or drink in case he needs an anaesthetic later.

CHOKING

If the baby is having trouble breathing or makes a noise when he draws breath and you have no evidence that he has swallowed anything, then don't interfere in any way but get him seen by a doctor straight away.

This is very rare, but if he makes a loud noise on drawing breath and is drooling and unable to swallow he may have an infection of the epiglottis. Sit him up and lean him forward and get him to a doctor or hospital fast. Don't interfere in any way unless he actually stops breathing when you must try mouth-to-mouth (see page 119).

Choking on an object

If you strongly suspect the baby has swallowed or inhaled something (food or any other foreign body), watch him carefully.

▦ If he can still breathe, cough or talk, then don't interfere – leave well alone and if he's old enough, encourage him to cough. The power of the cough is far greater than anything you can do, producing four or five times more pressure than a chest thrust.

If he is having difficulty breathing and can no longer cough, don't waste time trying to get the object out other than gently clearing his mouth with your finger – do as follows:

Small baby:

▦ Lie him face down along your arm which is braced against your body, his head tilted downwards and supported by your hand firmly holding his jaw.

▦ Bang him sharply high between the shoulder blades four times with the heel of your hand.

Toddler or large baby:

▦ Put him over your knee, tilted head down, and bang him sharply high between the shoulder blades about four times with the heel of your hand.

▦ If this doesn't work, place your free hand on baby's back so he is sandwiched between two hands.

▦ While continuing to support his head and neck, turn him over as a unit and place him on your thigh, his head lower than his trunk, and perform four chest thrusts as follows:

▦ Feel for the bottom of his ribs and find where they join in the middle at the bottom of his breastbone. Measure one finger's breadth above this place so you are over the lower part of the breastbone.

▦ With two or three fingers, depending on his size, press down firmly but not jerkily to a depth of 1–2 cm/½–1 in, letting the chest come up again after each push, but not taking your fingers off.

░ Do four of these chest thrusts.

░ Open baby's mouth by grasping both the tongue and lower jaw between the thumb and finger and lifting. Check in his mouth to see if there is anything easily removable, but don't just stick your finger blindly down his throat – that may make things worse.

If he is still unable to breathe, you must start mouth-to-mouth breathing.

░ First open his airway. Let his head tilt back, supported on your hand, and lift the bony part of his chin with your other hand. Keeping his head tilted back to maintain an open airway, place your mouth to cover baby's nose and mouth (or if he's too big, pinch his nose shut and just cover his mouth with yours). Blow gently into his mouth, watching to see that his chest rises. Stop as soon as you see it do so – don't over-inflate. If his chest does not rise, reposition his head and check the airway is open. Do one more breath. If his chest still does not rise, turn him over and do as follows.

░ Four more back blows.

░ Then four more chest thrusts.

░ Then two more breaths.

░ Repeat this sequence until help arrives or the baby starts breathing on his own.

A TO Z OF EMERGENCIES AND WHAT TO DO

Remember this is not a health-care manual; listed here you will only find conditions that are potential emergencies – or those you might think are so. If anything worries you about the health of your baby, check with your doctor.

You'll be able to handle an emergency much better if you've learnt first aid on a proper course. It doesn't take long and will give you great peace of mind. The British Red Cross Society, or St John Ambulance Brigade (St Andrew's Ambulance Association if you live in Scotland) run excellent first-aid courses. Headquarters are listed under *Useful Addresses*, page 170, and you can contact your local branch of the organization by looking it up in the telephone book.

ARM

If your toddler's arm suddenly looks paralysed and he can't use it, don't worry – he hasn't had a stroke! He may have a *pulled elbow*. This can happen very easily if his arm is jerked and twisted while being pulled along or played with for instance.

Take him to your doctor or local hospital where they will easily twist it and put it back into its normal position.

BIRTH – EMERGENCY

If the baby is born away from medical help and he comes out crying – fine.

■ Leave the cord still attached. Don't wash him, just dry him with a towel, wrap him warmly and place on the mother's tummy.

■ Get them both to hospital quickly, dialling 999 for an ambulance if necessary.

If the baby doesn't cry or breathe, slap him two or three times on the soles of the feet, then dry him gently and wrap him up quickly. Keep him warm.

■ If he still isn't breathing, try gentle mouth-to-mouth breathing (see page 119).

BLEEDING

See page 126.

BREATH-HOLDING

As the ultimate protest at the end of a tantrum a toddler will sometimes hold his breath so long that he goes blue in the face and eventually becomes unconscious. This can be very frightening, but is nothing to worry about. Immediately he loses consciousness he will begin to breathe again and will be none the worse for wear.

The calmer and less concerned you can appear to be the more quickly he will abandon this upsetting habit.

If he doesn't immediately regain consciousness within a second or two, you must proceed as for *Unconsciousness* (see page 163).

BREATHING – STOPPED

See *B – Breathing*, page 119.

BRUISES

Bruises are a normal part of a young child's life and normally need no treatment. If applied quickly, a cold compress or ice pack (ice cubes in a polythene bag, wrapped in a cloth) may help to prevent swelling and relieve pain.

■ If a child has fallen badly and is extensively bruised, you should contact your doctor as he may wish to check for any possible fractures (see *Falls and knocks*, page 142).

■ Many parents worry because their child seems to bruise very easily. There is almost certainly no reason to be concerned, but as there are some medical conditions of which bruising is a sign, you should check with your doctor if you are worried.

BURNS AND SCALDS

■ Don't put anything on the burn, such as butter, grease or antiseptic cream.

■ Get to cold water fast and immerse the burn in it for at least ten minutes. This is to cool it down as quickly as possible and stop more burning. Ignore the baby's screams or protestations: this really is the best thing for him and will soothe the pain as well as preventing further tissue damage. Either put the burnt part under the tap, letting the water trickle gently over it, or submerge it in a bowl, basin or the bath. Change the water frequently or keep the tap running so that it stays cold. Alternatively, cover the burn with wet towels.

■ Take off clothes where necessary to let water get to skin, but don't try to remove any burnt clothing: it will be sterile in any case.

■ If the baby has swallowed something too hot and has burnt his mouth and throat, give him sips of cold water or milk to cool it. If he has put the spout of a hot kettle or teapot in his mouth, he must be seen by a doctor as there may be scalding of the mouth.

■ Anything other than a very small burn must be seen by a doctor. An area about the size of your hand needs to be treated at hospital.

■ If the burns are bad and/or his throat is swelling, get him to hospital and watch his breathing carefully. Shout for someone to dial your doctor or 999 for an ambulance or for someone to drive you to hospital – don't leave the child yourself or move him from the cold water.

■ If you're alone, cool the burn first before telephoning.

■ While waiting for help, take off anything tight like a belt or bracelet and undo tight clothing: there may be swelling.

■ After cooling, cover the burn lightly with some clean, smooth cotton material such as a pillow case, handkerchief or tea towel to help prevent infection. Soak it well in clean water first, as this helps prevent evaporation of fluid from the burn and is easier and less painful to remove later.

■ Don't prick any blisters. The liquid inside a blister is sterile; by bursting it you could slow down healing and let in infection.

■ Keep the baby warm and talk to him soothingly and reassuringly until help arrives.

CAT SCRATCHES

Wash the wounds well with soap and water. As cat scratches tend to be superficial, there is no need for tetanus treatment.

CHOKING

See page 127.

COLD INJURY

This is not the same as hypothermia: cold injury, which includes such things as frostbite, affects parts of the body rather than the whole body. If the baby has been exposed to very cold weather and has become drowsy, lethargic and will not eat, he may possibly be suffering from cold injury.

■ Don't be fooled by very pink, healthy-looking hands and face: feel his skin. If it is cold, take him quickly to your doctor or A and E department. Cuddle him and add extra wraps, but don't use any external heat such as a hot bath to try to warm him rapidly – it could be dangerous. He must be warmed up slowly.

CONCUSSION

This is a temporary disturbance of the brain – a kind of 'brain-shaking', which can be caused by a blow to the head. If your child has banged his head but has no external wound, you should watch him for any changes in behaviour and levels of consciousness – in other words, how alert he is. Other things to watch for include headaches, clumsiness, weakness or one pupil larger than another. If you notice anything like this, take the child to hospital. They won't necessarily take an X-ray (see also *Head injuries*, page 149).

COUGHING

Most coughs are viral and will not need any treatment, but always have your baby checked.

■ If he is coughing and choking and having difficulty breathing, see *Choking* (page 127).

■ Coughing may result from swallowing white spirit or corrosive fluid. If you suspect he has swallowed some, don't try to make him sick – telephone your doctor or get him to hospital quickly, dialling 999 for an ambulance, if necessary, and taking a sample of the fluid with you.

■ If baby develops croup – a hoarse noisy cough with difficulty in drawing breath – he should be seen by a doctor. You may be able to give him some immediate relief by holding him near (but not too near) a hot shower or boiling kettle (don't let it boil dry). Damp air helps to ease a dry cough. Sit the child on your knee in this humid environment and reassure him. Telephone your doctor and make sure he comes to see the baby as quickly as possible.

■ If he is making a loud noise while he breathes and is *drooling badly* and apparently unable to swallow, get him to a doctor as quickly as possible, calling 999 for an ambulance if necessary, as he might have an infection of the epiglottis. This is *very rare* but if it happens don't try mouth-to-mouth until absolutely necessary, as you might make the throat go into spasm and close up completely.

CUTS

■ Take out any easily removable pieces of glass or foreign bodies, but do not pull out anything deeply embedded – you might release heavy bleeding which is being stemmed by the foreign body. If there is heavy bleeding, see page 126.

■ Stop any slight bleeding by pressing hard on the wound with your fingers or a piece of freshly laundered cloth or handkerchief soaked in clean water. Raise the wound above the level of the heart if possible.

■ Minor cuts should be rinsed thoroughly under a running tap, then cleaned with gentle strokes away from the wound with cotton wool, soap and water. Dry and apply a sticky plaster.

■ If the wound is deep it may need stitching, so check with your local A and E department. These days sticky strips are often used instead of stitches to bring the skin together. (It is essential that the skin meets in a bad cut to prevent infection entering the wound.)

■ If the baby or toddler bites his tongue badly, it is unlikely to need any stitches – even ragged-looking cuts heal well – but if the bleeding won't stop, ring your doctor or get him to hospital.

DEHYDRATION

If a baby is vomiting frequently and/or has diarrhoea, there may be a danger of his losing too much fluid. This can happen very quickly in babies.

■ If you think your baby is losing more fluid than he is taking in, you should immediately give him a solution of Rehidrat or Dioralyte and then seek medical help.

See also *Diarrhoea*, below.

DIARRHOEA

■ If baby has frequent watery motions (diarrhoea), he must be seen by a doctor. While you are waiting, make sure he has plenty to drink to replace lost fluid. A solution of Rehidrat or Dioralyte is best, but give small quantities frequently to prevent it being vomited back.

■ If he is also vomiting, he must be seen urgently, as the two together can lead to dehydration and he may need treatment. If in doubt take him to a doctor or hospital quickly, if necessary calling an ambulance.

■ If he becomes very weak while waiting for help, or on the way to hospital, watch his A–B–C (see page 116).

■ If there is any blood in his motions, take him to your doctor or to hospital.

■ If there is any blood in his motions and he is vomiting and screaming, get him to hospital as quickly as you can.

DOG BITES

■ Stop any bleeding (see page 126).

■ Clean the wound thoroughly with soap and water.

■ Take him to a doctor or hospital: he may need an anti-tetanus injection, or, in extremely rare cases, a rabies inoculation.

DROWNING

■ If baby is not breathing, start mouth-to-mouth breathing immediately – even in the water if necessary (see A–B–C, page 119).

■ Don't waste too much time trying to get water out of his lungs or throat – let the most obvious water pour out and then give mouth-to-mouth.

■ Shout for someone to call an ambulance, or drive you to hospital while you continue resuscitation.

■ If the water was very cold, get someone to wrap him in a blanket to insulate him. Don't try to warm him up – at this stage it is unnecessary and may even be counterproductive.

■ If you're on your own, keep breathing for him and doing heart compressions if necessary until he breathes on his own. Don't give up – even if he appears completely lifeless.

■ You must keep going until you reach hospital or help arrives: children who have been submerged in cold water for as long as 30 to 40 minutes have survived, sometimes after hours of mouth-to-mouth breathing.

EARS

An object pushed into the ear rarely does any harm, but trying to get it out often does.

■ If the baby has pushed something into his ear, don't try to get it out, even if it looks easy. By doing so you may make the baby jump and cause the object – perhaps a hairgrip or ballpoint pen top – to go deeper into the ear and scratch or possibly perforate the ear drum, causing permanent damage. This is not an emergency but you should take him to your doctor or casualty department.

■ Any bleeding from the ear should be seen by a doctor, especially after a head injury (see page 149). Never plug the ear, but cover it lightly with a pad of material or clean handkerchief while waiting for the ambulance or while taking him to hospital.

■ If the baby has been crying more than usual, is very fretful and keeps touching or holding his ear, he may have an ear infection. This must be checked by a doctor as an ear infection left untreated can result in permanent damage to the ear drum. Telephone your doctor who may advise you to give paracetamol to relieve the pain until the baby can be seen.

ELECTRIC SHOCK

■ Do not touch the baby before you have switched off the electricity at source.

■ If this is not possible, insulate yourself by standing on a rubber surface or on thick layers of dry cloth or newspapers and pull baby away from contact with a dry broom handle, a piece of rope or by his dry clothing – don't touch anything damp or metallic.

■ Check baby's A–B–C (see page 116).

■ Check and treat any burns (see page 132).

■ Get baby to a doctor or hospital quickly, calling for an ambulance if necessary.

EYES

If you think the baby has something in his eye, treat it very carefully.

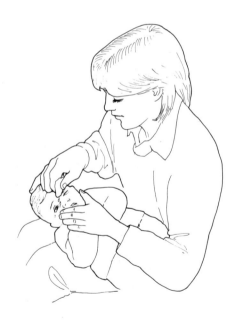

■ Lean baby's head back, pull the lower lid down very gently and trickle a little clean (preferably boiled and cooled) water over his eye to clean it out. If this doesn't work and you can see the foreign body easily then very gently flick it out with the wetted corner of a clean handkerchief or piece of cloth.

■ If it continues to bother him badly and you suspect it may be something sharp, take him quickly to your doctor or if necessary the A and E department. If you have an eye patch you can tape it over the eye with sellotape or plaster, but don't improvise by covering the eye with cotton wool or anything else.

■ If an object is stuck into the eye itself, get him quickly to hospital or doctor, using an ambulance if necessary. Don't put any pressure on the eye. If he tries to touch his eye, cover it with something like part of a paper cup taped over.

■ If the baby has splashed his eyes with a household, garden or cosmetic liquid, hold his head gently back over a sink or

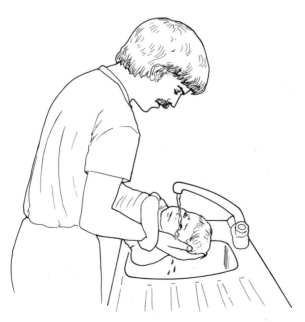

basin and pour clean water continuously over his eyes to wash them out. Do this for at least 10 minutes, and then get him to hospital or doctor, using an ambulance if necessary.

◼ Always take baby to your doctor if he has any redness in the eyes or any discharge – eyes are precious.

◼ A stye is not an emergency and requires no treatment.

FALLS AND KNOCKS

◼ If the baby is lying on the floor, pick him up gently as a unit, without twisting or bending his body, and put him in a safe place where you can take a good look at him. Don't be frightened to move him: babies tend to 'bounce', and it is unlikely he has done major damage. It is very unusual for bad breaks to occur.

If baby is unconscious, check A–B–C immediately (see page 116).

If he is breathing but unconscious or lethargic

◼ Get someone to phone for your doctor or ambulance.

◼ Stop any bleeding (see page 126).

◼ Gently roll him over on to his tummy until help arrives, taking care not to twist his body. Don't break the natural contour of his spine and keep his neck in one line in case of any injury. It is most unlikely his spine has been significantly injured but be careful of his neck: it could be damaged even if he is still breathing. Check his airway.

■ Keep him covered and warm, but not too hot, until help arrives. Keep checking his airway is clear and that he is breathing.

■ If there is any bleeding from the ear, do not plug it with anything. Cover it lightly with a pad of material or handkerchief while you wait for help, or while taking him to hospital.

■ Do not give the baby anything to eat or drink, or any painkillers, in case he needs an anaesthetic later.

If the baby is breathing and alert

■ If he is fully conscious and responsive, take a look at him: is any limb obviously deformed or useless?

■ Is there marked swelling anywhere?

■ If there is any obvious deformity, do not disturb the injured part any further.

■ If you have to move him, support and immobilize the injured part with a sling or your hands, keeping it in the position the baby seems to find most comfortable. Don't worry – all fractures in young children heal. Even completely unnoticed fractures will usually resolve themselves and if there is any deformity it will often remodel with growth.

■ If there is no obvious deformity and everything looks normal, pick him up and cuddle him. He will probably be perfectly all right: babies can fall from surprising heights and suffer no damage.

■ If in any doubt, take him to your doctor or A and E department to have him checked. You must take him if he has been unconscious, or the injury looks serious, or he has had a bad bang to his head (see *Head injuries*, page 149).

FINGERS – TRAPPED OR CRUSHED

Don't panic! Most crushed fingers heal perfectly well without any treatment and nearly every child has suffered this accident to some degree. Almost certainly the fingers will need no stitching. The doctor may apply special sticky strips – rather like tiny pieces of sticky tape – to hold the wound together while it heals. Nails hanging off may have to be removed but will grow again. The fingers will look awful at the first dressing but after a few weeks will begin to look perfectly normal. A day or two after treatment, encourage the baby to move them as much as possible.

■ Reassure your frightened toddler.

■ Plunge the fingers into cold water for five minutes to reduce pain and swelling, then cover them gently with a piece of clean cloth, such as a freshly laundered tea towel or handkerchief.

■ If there is an open wound, dampen the cloth with clean water before covering the fingers as it will be easier and less painful for the doctor to remove later.

■ Raise the injured hand to help prevent swelling and make it more comfortable; put it in a sling if possible.

■ Take him to your doctor or A and E department.

■ Don't give him anything to eat or drink or any painkillers in case he needs an anaesthetic at the hospital.

FINGERTIP AMPUTATED

■ Cover the wounded finger with a piece of clean, damp cloth, such as a freshly laundered tea towel or handkerchief, and take the baby to hospital, taking the fingertip with you. It may be possible to stitch it back on again.

Believe it or not, if the amputation is between the first joint of the finger and the nail, the tip will re-grow on a child up to about the age of three (including the nail) and function normally!

FIRE

■ Close the door of the room where the fire is. This will help delay the spread of fire and smoke. The average door should withstand a fire for 10 to 15 minutes (20 minutes if it's very solid).

■ Get everyone out of the house. If you live in a flat, don't use the lift. Just go – don't try to put out the fire, or collect valuables. Shut all doors and windows if you safely can.

■ Dial 999 for the fire brigade from a neighbour's house or a phone box.

If you are cut off by fire

■ Dial 999 for the fire brigade if you can.

■ Go to the window, open or smash it and call for help. There is no need to go into elaborate escape procedures if your shouts have been heard. Very often people jump from windows, breaking bones in the process, when if they'd waited a few minutes longer, the fire brigade would have been there. Don't panic!

■ If possible, try to get everyone in the same room – ideally parents should go to the children's room.

■ Close the door and put a blanket, coat or rug along the bottom of the door to stop smoke coming in.

■ Gather near the open window and wait for the fire brigade to arrive.

■ If the room becomes smoky, stay low. It's easier to breathe.

The fire prevention officers stress that none of the following escape procedures should be tried unless absolutely essential.

■ If you really *have* to get out (flames licking round your ankles), throw cushions, bedding or a mattress on to the ground outside.

■ If you have smashed the window remove jagged glass from the lower sill and cover it with a blanket.

■ Get out feet first and lower yourself to your fingertips before dropping to the ground.

■ Do not throw children from higher than the first floor. Ideally one adult should go out first and try to catch small children lowered by another adult.

■ A child who has been in a burning house must be taken to hospital immediately, even if there is no evidence of burns, as there may be damage to his airway and lungs.

Child's clothes on fire

■ Don't let the child run – this fans the flames and increases burns dramatically.

■ Make him lie down on the floor and roll him around to douse the flames. Alternatively, smother the flames with a blanket or rug.

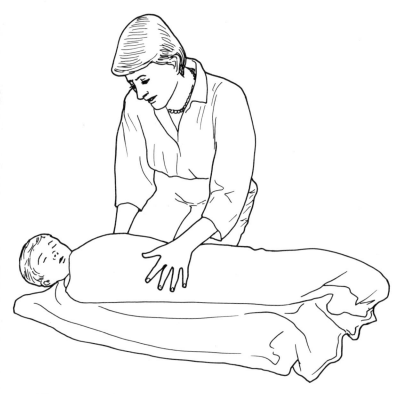

■ Treat any burns (see page 132).

Burning fat on stove

■ Turn off the heat.

■ Don't try to move the pan.

■ Don't put water into it.

■ Cover it quickly with a fire blanket, wet cloth or lid. Leave it to cool.

Small fires

■ Smother quickly with a fire blanket or rug. If your first attempt is unsuccessful, leave the room immediately, shutting the door if you can.

(See also *Prevention*, pages 24–29.)

FITS OR CONVULSIONS

The signs of a fit or convulsion are a rigidity of the body followed by relaxing and clenching muscles so that the baby jerks and twitches. They are usually caused by a very high temperature (associated with a variety of illnesses), though they can result from fright or occasionally temper. They may also be caused by poisoning. If you suspect the baby has swallowed something, dial 999 for an ambulance and if possible take a sample of what he has swallowed with you to hospital. Do not try to make him sick.

Although fits seem frightening they are not dangerous. The only danger would come from his being left alone and either inhaling vomit or injuring himself while thrashing about.

■ Make sure there is nothing within reach that the baby can bang himself against.

■ Turn him gently on to his front if you can, with his head turned to one side.

■ Don't wrap him – undress him if you can, but don't over cool him.

■ Hold him gently if possible and keep calm – the fit will probably stop of its own accord.

■ Cool him by sponging with tepid (not ice-cold) water. Let it dry on his skin.

■ Check his A–B–C (see page 116).

■ If he is breathing, check his position again. He should be on his tummy with his head turned to one side. Tilt his head back so his airway is clear. Make sure his mouth and nose are clear of any sick or froth. Check his breathing again.

■ Even if the fit has stopped, contact your doctor.

■ If the fit continues, get baby to your doctor or hospital as quickly as possible, if necessary calling an ambulance.

HEAD INJURIES

See *Falls and knocks*, page 142, for immediate action.

Don't panic – most babies have a bang on the head at one time or another and it's unlikely he's done any serious damage.

■ Any bad bang to the head must be seen by a doctor – take him to your doctor or A and E department.

■ Any bleeding from the scalp is almost a good sign – better than a bad bang where the bleeding may be happening internally. Have him checked by your doctor in case the wound needs a stitch.

■ Continued bleeding or leakage of clear fluid from an ear must be taken seriously and be seen by a doctor.

■ Babies and young children can produce alarming lumps on the forehead after a bang on the head. This is bleeding under the scalp and doesn't mean anything sinister like brain damage. It probably needs no treatment, but any swelling in the scalp should be seen by a doctor: there may be a fracture of the skull underneath.

■ When you leave the hospital after treatment for a head injury and the hospital feels the baby may develop signs of concussion (see page 135), you'll be given a card telling you what to watch out for. To be on the safe side you should gently wake your baby or toddler every three hours or so to check his condition the night after a head injury.

■ The hospital will tell you to contact your doctor or the hospital immediately in the event of:

1. Extreme difficulty in waking your child.
2. Change in his colour.
3. Noisy, funny breathing. If he's snoring it must not be considered a deep, peaceful sleep – it could be dangerous. Shake him gently to see if he will wake.
4. A squint, or differently sized pupils.
5. Being sick repeatedly.
6. Continuous, unusual, unexplained crying.

■ If in any doubt, ring your doctor or the hospital.

(See also *Bruises*, page 132.)

HEART – STOPPED

See C – *Circulation*, page 120.

HIGH TEMPERATURE

There are wide variations in what can be considered a 'normal' temperature for a baby. Officially the normal temperature is 36.9°C/98.4°F, but a baby's temperature can swoop up and down very easily; even running around can raise it a degree or so.

■ If you suspect the baby is hotter than usual, take his temperature with the thermometer under his arm – never in his mouth. There are new electronic digital thermometers which are very reliable and don't break if you drop them.

■ Alternatively, you may know your baby's normal temperature well enough to judge if he is feverish by feeling the back of his neck or his forehead with your hand. Some parents find it easy to tell if they press their lips on the baby's forehead.

■ Use your common sense in deciding whether to call the doctor. If his temperature is only slightly up and he doesn't seem otherwise unwell, you may wish to give your child some paracetamol-based syrup to bring down his temperature; but if he is clearly ill, let your doctor know.

■ If he has a really high temperature (over about 39°C/103°F) call your doctor. Meanwhile sponge him with tepid water to bring down his temperature and make him more comfortable.

■ If his natural inclination is to push back the covers, let him do so.

■ Don't worry – a baby's temperature can soar dramatically with no serious cause and no ill effect. However, a high temperature should always be checked by a doctor.

HYPOTHERMIA

This condition (not to be confused with *Cold injury*, page 134) can occur if the baby has been exposed to very cold conditions or has accidentally been immersed in cold water. If he is lethargic and drowsy and feels very cold to touch, his temperature may have dropped dangerously low. Don't be fooled by pink, healthy-looking cheeks – he may still be too cold.

■ Telephone for a doctor or ambulance.

■ Move the baby to a warm room, but do not apply direct heat of any kind. The aim is to warm him up *gradually*.

■ Cover the baby to prevent any further heat loss.

LETHARGY – DROWSINESS, WON'T WAKE

■ If baby is unusually drowsy or floppy or doesn't seem to know you, get him to a doctor or hospital urgently, calling an ambulance if necessary. On the way watch his A–B–C (see page 116).

■ Drowsiness, particularly in an ill baby, must always be taken seriously.

■ Drowsiness is sometimes a symptom of poisoning. If he has swallowed something, do not try to make him sick; take a sample of what he has swallowed with you to hospital.

NOSE

Blocked nose

■ If baby has difficulty breathing through his nose, try cleaning it gently with a wet cotton bud. If he still has trouble, take him to your doctor.

■ It will make it difficult for him to feed if he cannot breathe through his nose while sucking. Some babies are less efficient than others at breathing through their mouths when their noses are blocked. If baby is in any way struggling to breathe, take him urgently to your doctor or hospital, watching his A–B–C (see page 116) meanwhile.

■ Bear in mind the possibility he may have pushed something up his nostril (see page 154).

Nose bleeds

■ Nose bleeds caused by a blow on the head should be seen by a doctor (see *Head injuries*, page 149).

■ Other nose bleeds usually mean nothing serious. Do not plug the nose. Gently sit baby up, head leaning slightly forward, and pinch his nostrils shut for between two and ten minutes (or as long as an active baby will let you!).

■ If bleeding has stopped, leave well alone. Don't pick at any clots or wipe his nose. Distract the baby if he is trying to fiddle with his nose.

■ If bleeding continues or nose bleeds are frequent, take him to your doctor or hospital, calling an ambulance if necessary.

Object pushed up nose

This is not an emergency, but if the object doesn't come out after trying the following, you should take your baby to your doctor or hospital.

■ Don't try to get the object out by poking a cotton bud up his nostril; you may well push it further up and do some damage.

■ If you can see the object, apply pressure behind it so he doesn't sniff and draw it further in.

■ If he is old enough, ask him to blow his nose, holding the empty nostril closed.

OBJECT SWALLOWED

■ If baby has swallowed something you think may be poisonous, see page 155.

■ If he has swallowed something and is coughing and distressed, it may have stuck in his food pipe. Take him to your doctor or A and E department and tell them what he has swallowed.

■ If he is choking, something may have gone down the 'wrong way' into the windpipe – see *Choking*, page 127.

■ If he has swallowed a smooth, small object, other than a battery (see below), but seems quite happy and is not choking or otherwise distressed, just let nature take its course until it comes out the other end!

■ If you are unsure, telephone your doctor's surgery for advice. About 80–90 per cent of foreign bodies pass through the stomach with no problems but some do not and may have to be removed.

■ The small round batteries that are used in pocket computer games and independent heated hair-stylers may leak if swallowed. Get him to hospital and take a similar battery with you, or the toy from which it came, or even the toy instructions, so the doctors can identify the contents of the battery.

■ If he has swallowed something sharp, it may well pass right through but you mustn't risk it – take him to your doctor or A and E department.

■ Whatever he has swallowed, don't try to make him sick.

POISONING

■ Whatever has been swallowed, never try to make the baby sick by using salt and water or any other method. It can be dangerous.

■ If he is sick of his own accord, keep a sample of the vomit to show to the doctors later.

■ Try to note down the time the poison was swallowed: this may be vital information for the doctors later.

■ Don't be misled if there are no symptoms – some poisons, such as iron, take several hours to show effect, and treatment is urgent.

■ If you are unsure as to whether he has swallowed something or not, telephone your doctor or local A and E department; they may be able to reassure you over the telephone or they may ask you to take him to hospital to be on the safe side – there are many dangerous pills which would not show any immediate effect on the baby.

Household or garden chemicals

■ Gently persuade him to drink a glass of milk or water to dilute the poison.

■ If he is not suffering any apparent ill-effects, quickly telephone your doctor or A and E department to ask their advice. He may need no treatment.

■ If he is screaming, coughing, having convulsions or behaving strangely in any way, take him straight to hospital, dialling 999 for an ambulance if necessary. Also take a sample of the liquid and the container from which he drank.

■ If he has swallowed paraffin or white spirit (turps substitute) give him some milk. It is especially important not to try to make him sick. Take him to hospital, taking a sample of the liquid and the container from which he drank.

Medicine, or pills

■ Do your best to find out exactly what your child has taken and how much, and telephone your doctor or local A and E department immediately; they may be able to reassure you over the telephone and save a distressing visit to hospital.

■ If you do have to take him to hospital (dialling 999 for an ambulance if necessary), take a sample of what he has swallowed with you as well as the container which should have the name printed on it.

■ Do not try to make him sick, but if he vomits of his own accord, have a good look at it to see how many pills or capsules he has brought up. Try to take a sample of the vomit with you to the hospital.

Alcohol

■ If more than a few mouthfuls of spirits or fortified wine have been swallowed, it can be dangerous. Get your baby to a doctor. Remember – what may be harmless to you may be poisonous to your baby.

PULLED ELBOW

See *Arm*, page 130.

RASH

■ A red rash with little white bumps that look like nettle stings may be an allergic reaction to something the baby has eaten. This is rare but if it does happen, watch for swelling, particularly around his mouth; if his throat starts to swell, it could be dangerous.

■ If you don't know what has caused it, you should always see your doctor. It may well be one of the common infectious diseases of childhood. Although very few rashes indicate anything serious, you should always consult your doctor if you cannot pinpoint the cause. A rash can be a symptom of meningitis and, though this is rare, a delay in diagnosis can be fatal.

ROAD ACCIDENTS – PEDESTRIAN

■ Shout for someone to dial 999 for an ambulance.

■ If you suspect any broken bones, don't move him unless absolutely necessary – if he is in the middle of the road for instance.

■ Check A–B–C (see page 116), then try to stop any serious bleeding (see page 126).

■ Don't give the baby anything to eat or drink in case he needs an anaesthetic later.

SCALDS

See *Burns and scalds*, page 132.

SCREAMING OR PROLONGED CRYING

Go through the following checklist before you assume something is seriously wrong with your baby.

■ **Bee sting**. Look for a small red bump – if it looks as if he's been stung, treat as *Stings*, page 162.

■ **Cold.** If he feels chilly, wrap him well and cuddle him to warm him.

■ **Colic.** If he pulls his legs into his tummy and appears to have griping pains, he may be suffering from colic. Walk up and down with him reassuringly until it passes. Wind can sometimes be caused by too small a hole in the teat; try using a larger one. If colic happens frequently and badly, see your doctor.

■ **Hot.** If he feels hot to touch, try taking a layer of clothes off or sponge him with tepid water.

■ **Hungry.** Try to calm him and feed him.

■ **Lonely.** Has he been left alone and got himself 'in a state'? Cuddle him reassuringly.

■ **Overtired.** Try rocking him gently and calmly to sleep.

■ **Poisoning.** Could he have swallowed something corrosive? If you suspect this, see page 155.

■ **Teething.** Have a look in his mouth; if his gum has a red swelling (or even a little white corner peeping through) it could be a tooth about to erupt. Rub the gums firmly with your clean fingertip or give him something hard and cold to bite on, such as a water-filled teether (keep it in the fridge so that it's chilled and ready to use).

■ **Thirsty.** In hot weather babies need water as well as milk.

■ **Uncomfortable.** Clothing too tight? Nappy pin sticking in? Dirty nappy?

■ If you think none of these things is the cause but he still cries more than usual or inconsolably, see your doctor. It may turn out to be a throat or ear infection, or some other medical condition.

■ If he is obviously in great distress and pain, get him to a doctor or hospital quickly, if necessary calling an ambulance.

■ If he screams desperately, is vomiting and passing anything that looks like blood in his motions, get him to hospital as quickly as possible.

SHOCK

This term can be quite confusing. It doesn't mean simply that the baby is upset and frightened; it is a medical condition. Shock is often caused by blood or fluid loss. This can occur through illness involving diarrhoea or vomiting, or after an accident, such as a fall. Signs to look for are:

- Pale or grey skin
- Faintness
- Giddiness
- Clamminess
- Rapid breathing
- Restlessness
- Weakness

Minor shock (after a fright or fall)

■ Lie the child down on his tummy, with his head low and turned to the side.

■ Loosen any tight clothing.

■ Cover him with a coat or blanket, but don't try to warm him artificially with hot water bottles.

■ Talk to him calmly and reassuringly.

■ Don't give him anything to eat or drink until he is completely normal.

■ After five minutes or so he should return to normal or perhaps fall asleep. Don't leave him in case he vomits.

More serious shock (following an acute illness, allergic reaction or bad accident)

■ Get someone to telephone for a doctor.

■ Treat the child as for minor shock.

■ Don't leave him alone, and keep checking his A–B–C (see page 116).

SNAKE BITES

The adder is the only poisonous snake in Great Britain and is normally found on heathland. It is usually greyish with a wide, black zig-zag line along its back and black spots along its sides. Fortunately, the bite is rarely fatal.

■ After an adder bite, encourage the child to stay as still as possible – movement speeds the venom through the system.

■ Clean the bitten area thoroughly with water.

■ Apply a cold compress and keep the bitten limb still, tying it to the body if necessary.

■ Get your child to hospital quickly, calling an ambulance if necessary. He may be given an antidote to help recovery. The limb may swell up and turn blue, but all will be well in the end.

■ For non-poisonous snake bites, wash the bitten area thoroughly and then take the child to hospital as antibiotics or anti-tetanus may be necessary.

SPIN-DRYER INJURY

Sticking a hand into a spin-dryer which is still revolving can cause badly bruised, even broken, fingers and sometimes friction burns. These injuries must always be seen by a doctor as later swelling may be dangerous.

■ Treat the injured hand as for crushed fingers (see page 144).

■ Treat any friction burns (see *Burns and scalds*, page 132).

STINGS

Wasp, bee or jellyfish stings need no special treatment with acid, alkali or anything else.

■ Remove the sting from a bee sting with a pair of tweezers or by scraping it away with your fingernail.

■ Apply a cold compress to soothe and reduce swelling, or plunge the stung area into cold water. A lump of ice (or even an ice-cream) pressed against it can be very comforting. Local anaesthetic sprays can take away some of the pain, but doctors disagree about their value. Some research has indicated that they can provoke adverse reactions.

■ If your child has a severe allergic reaction to stings (swelling and redness, particularly around the mouth), take him to hospital as quickly as possible as his throat may swell. On the way, watch his A–B–C (see page 116).

STRANGE BEHAVIOUR – DIZZINESS, UNSTEADY WALKING

This can be a sign of poisoning with sleeping tablets, anti-depressants, travel-sickness tablets, alcohol or antifreeze.

■ Get him to hospital quickly, dialling 999 for an ambulance if necessary and taking a sample of what he has swallowed with you, or the container from which it came.

■ Do not try to make the baby sick, but if he vomits of his own accord, take the vomit with you to hospital so the doctors can see how much he has brought up.

SUNBURN

This should be avoided at all costs but if it does happen, treat as an ordinary burn, see page 132.

SUNSTROKE

This is very serious. Give your child a solution of Rehidrat or Dioralyte and seek medical help immediately.

TOES – CRUSHED

Treat exactly as for crushed fingers (see page 144).

UNCONSCIOUSNESS

- Try to stimulate baby by picking him up. Shout his name and gently shake him.
- If there is no response, keep calm.
- Call for someone to dial 999 for an ambulance or if necessary carry the baby to the telephone and dial yourself while starting the A–B–C procedure (see page 116).

VOMITING

Small amounts of regurgitated milk are nothing to worry about, but real vomiting, particularly if repeated or of a greenish colour or blood-stained, should not be ignored and the baby must be seen by a doctor.

■ Do not lie the baby on his back if he is being sick – he could choke. Sit him up leaning forward and support his head and tummy, or at least turn him on his side.

■ If vomiting is also accompanied by frequent watery motions (diarrhoea) he must be seen by your doctor quickly, as the two together can lead to excessive fluid loss and he may become dehydrated and need treatment. If in doubt, take him either to your doctor or hospital, calling an ambulance if necessary. (See *Diarrhoea*, page 137.)

■ If he is vomiting and passing anything that looks like blood in his motions and is screaming desperately, get him to hospital as quickly as possible.

■ If he is becoming very weak while you are waiting for help, or on the way to hospital, watch his A–B–C (see page 116).

WHEEZING

■ If your baby starts making wheezy noises and is having difficulty in breathing, talk calmly and reassuringly to him and take him to your doctor or A and E department as soon as possible. It is unlikely to be dangerous but he must be seen.

■ If prolonged and continuous wheezing suddenly starts in a toddler who has never wheezed before, he may possibly have inhaled something. This is not an emergency unless he is having difficulty breathing, but you must check with your doctor.

III.

USEFUL INFORMATION

APPROVED EQUIPMENT

The equipment mentioned in this book can be bought from major babycare shops, catalogue showrooms, ironmongers and department stores throughout the UK. Where possible, the British Standards number and an approximate price or price range are quoted.

Anti-slamming device, £2.50
Baby alarm, £19–£30
Baby bath and stand, £7–£15
Baby nest, BS 6595, £12.20
Baby walker, BS 4648, £16–£25
Bed guard, £13
Booster cushion (for car), £10–£14
Bouncing cradle, £9–£20
Bunk beds, £100–£200
Car roller blinds, £10
Car shade screens, £2.99
Carry-cot, BS 3881, £20–£60
Carry-cot restraint, BS AU 186, £10.50–£15
Cat net, £2

Changing table (with storage unit),   £55–£65
Chemical lavatory for dogs,   £20
Childproof car locks, AU 209, (priced according to make and model of car)
Childproof catches,   35p–45p each
Childproof medicine cabinet,   £35; lockable cabinet,   £18–£52; concealed cabinet,   £85
Child-resistant containers, BS 6652 or BS 5321
Child safety seat, BS 3254 or EEC regulation 44,   £20–£40
Christmas-tree lights, BS 4647,   £4–£10
Circuit-breaker,   £17–£19
Continental quilt (cot size), BS 5335,   £6–£10
Corner protectors,   45p each
Cot, BS 1753,   £50–£100
Cot bumpers,   £5–£10
Cot mattress, BS 1877,   £11–£28
Dog guard rail,   £11–£24 (bars); £35–£40 (wire mesh)
Dog muzzle (Baskerville model),   £4.55–£9
Dummy, BS 5239,   50p–70p
Dummy socket covers,   £1.15 for six
Fire blanket, BS 6575,   £10–£15
Fire guard, BS 6539 (open fires),   £18; BS 1945 (gas, electric & paraffin fires),   £23
Fridge lock,   £1.50–£3
Harness, BS 6684,   £3.50
Highchair, BS 5799,   £28–£55
Hob guard,   £12–£15
Infant carrier, rear-facing, BS AU 202,   £28–£40
Lavatory door lock,   £10.95
Lavatory lid lock,   £4
Low-flammability nightwear, BS 5722

Non-slip bath mat,   £6–£7
Paraffin heater, BS 3300,   £50–£80
Pillow, BS 1877,   £3–£4
Playpen, BS 4863,   £50
Pram, BS 4139,   £70–£140
Pushchair/buggy, BS 4792,   £30–£105
Reins, BS 3785 or BS 6684,   £3.50
Safety film, BS 6206C,   £13 per 180 cm/6 ft roll
Safety gate/barrier, BS 4125,   £16–£27
Safety glass, BS 6206,   £53 per sq. metre
Safety heater, BS 3456,   £30
Safety plug, BS 1363,   65p
Seat belt, ECE 16,   £9–£18; child's, BS 3254,   £12
Smoke detector, battery operated, BS 5446,   £10–£18
Spark guard, BS 3248,   £10
Toys, BS 5665 or BS 3443
Water-filled teething ring, BS 5665,   £1.80
Window lock/minimum opening device,   £4

USEFUL ADDRESSES

SAFETY ORGANIZATIONS

British Battery Manufacturers Association
7 Buckingham Gate
London SW1E 6JS

British Red Cross Society (H.Q.)
9 Grosvenor Crescent
London SW1
(Tel: 01–235 3241)
Contact your local branch through the telephone book.

British Standards Institution
2 Park Street
London W1A 2BS
(Tel: 01–629 9000)

Child Accident Prevention Trust
75 Portland Place
London W1N 3AL
(Tel: 01–636 2545)

Consumers' Association
(publishers of *Which?*)
14 Buckingham Street
London WC2N 6DS
(Tel: 01–839 1222)

Royal Society for the Prevention of Accidents (RoSPA)
Cannon House
Priory Queensway
Birmingham B4 6BS
(Tel: 021–233 2461)

St Andrew's Ambulance Association (H.Q.)
21 St John's Street
Edinburgh EH8 8DG
(Tel: 031–556 8711, from 9 a.m. to 1 p.m.)
Contact your local branch through the telephone book.

St John Ambulance (H.Q.)
1 Grosvenor Crescent
London SW1X 7EF
(Tel: 01–235 5231)
Contact your local branch through the telephone book.

SOME MANUFACTURERS AND RETAILERS OF SAFETY EQUIPMENT

The Animal Behaviour Centre
(dog muzzles)
PO Box 23
Chertsey
Surrey KT16 QPU
(Tel: 0932–566696)

Boots the Chemist PLC
Nottingham, NG2 3AA
(Tel: 0602–418522)

Brent Components Ltd
(coiled flexes)
112a High Street
Harlesden
London NW10 4SL
(Tel: 01–965 3636)

Frithgate Luton Ltd
(car safety systems, mail order)
2 Jubilee Street
Luton
Beds. LU2 0EA
(Tel: 0582–22129)

Glass and Glazing Federation
(safety glass information)
44–48 Borough High Street
London SE1 1XP
(Tel: 01–403 7177)

Hago Products Ltd
(guards for gas-cylinder heaters)
Shripney Road
Bognor Regis
West Sussex PO22 9NH
(Tel: 0243–863131)

Heinz Baby Club
Vince Road
Diss
Norfolk IP22 3HH
(Tel: 0379–651981)

Kiddi-Proof Products Ltd
(child-resistant catches, fridge locks, lavatory locks)
Unit 1
65/67 Hagden Lane
Watford WD1 8NA
(Tel: 0923–225216)

Kiddymail
(baby specialist, mail order)
Vince Road
Diss
Norfolk IP22 3HH
(Tel: 0379–644720)

Kwik-Fit Euro
(child safety seats)
Temple Fields
Edinburgh Way
Harlow
Essex
(Tel: Freephone Kwik-Fit for your nearest branch)

Merrybabe Ltd
(folding gates)
Hirst House
Station Road
Edenbridge
Kent TN8 6EY
(Tel: 0732–865538)

Mothercare Customer Service Dept
Cherry Tree Road
Watford
Herts WD2 5SH
(Tel: 0923–31616)

Quickfit Safety Belt Service
(car safety systems)
39 Kenton Park Parade
Kenton Road
Harrow HA3 8DN
(Tel: 01–907 1162)

TRAVEL SAFETY INSURERS

Europ Assistance
(General 24-hour emergency service for
vehicles and personal insurance)
252 High St
Croydon
(Tel: 01–680 1234)

Mondial Assistance
Church House
Old Palace Road
Croydon
(Tel: 01–681 2525)

A NOTE TO THE READER

Jane Asher has talked to dozens of doctors, safety experts and parents of young children in order to cover as many aspects of child safety as possible in this book. If there is any safety information you feel should be included in the next edition, or if your child has been involved in an accident not mentioned here, please write to: Keep Your Baby Safe, Penguin Books Ltd, 27 Wrights Lane, London W8 5TZ.

Index

Note: references in **bold type** are to emergency action.

NAME: ....

DATE OF BIRTH: ....

ADDRESS: ....

....

....

TELEPHONE No.: ....

FATHER: ....

WORK No.: ....

MOTHER: ....

WORK No.: ....

DOCTOR: ....

ADDRESS: ....

....

....

TELEPHONE No.: ....

EMERGENCY No.: ....

NEAREST ACCIDENT AND EMERGENCY DEPT:

....

....

....

TELEPHONE No.: ....

ALLERGIES ETC.:

....

....

....

IMMUNIZATION RECORD

AGE	IMMUNIZATION AGAINST	DATE

N.H.S. NUMBER: